To, The forgetful Jim,
You are forgiven
Best wishes
Victoria Hillman

Forgotten Little Creatures

Redfern Natural History Productions
Poole, Dorset, England
www.redfernnaturalhistory.com

Forgotten Little Creatures
ISBN 978-1-908787-28-6

I would like say a huge "Thank you!" to all those that have encouraged me throughout this project and in producing the subsequent book. In particular, I thank my mum, dad, and my husband Chris, who have made me tea and patched me up after long days in the field, not to mention put up with 3am alarms!

I would also like to say thank you to all the wonderful people I have met along the way, many of whom have become friends, who helped me with equipment, locations and identifications, or joined me on some of the photographic outings and shared a giggle at getting ridiculously wet and muddy at times.

Last but by no means least, to all the wonderful plants and animals that I have had the pleasure of spending so much time with, thank you; may you continue to thrive in these wonderful habitats, protected by those that love you!

Contents

Victoria Hillman

I am a scientist by training with a BSc in Zoology with Marine Zoology from the University of Wales, Bangor and an MSc in Wildlife Biology and Conservation from Edinburgh Napier University. Although I have no formal qualifications in photography, I have always loved the outdoors and been fascinated by the natural world; from the moment my parents bought me my first camera, I have enjoyed taking photographs of all kinds of wildlife. Throughout my studies and the following years I worked on not only gaining knowledge of the natural world but also on my photography, learning how to make the most of my equipment and available light and even learning to develop and print my work using a darkroom.

While my studies have covered a wide range of species from both the marine and terrestrial environments, over the last few years my fascination has become concentrated on plants, invertebrates, amphibians and reptiles, especially for those species that are less loved or often overlooked.

My Photography Ethics

Ethical, truthful and responsible photography is something I feel very strongly about. The welfare of my subject is my main priority, closely followed by the integrity of its habitat. All my images are taken where I have found my subjects, working with what is in front of me and never moving them to better locations or gardening around them. I am very careful to cause as little disturbance as possible to both my subject and its environment, both by keeping a close eye on the subject for any signs of stress, or warnings that let me know if I accidentally get too close, and by taking care not to damage the habitat as I move around within it. I will spend weeks and months with just a handful of subjects at a time, learning as much as I can about them and how they interact with their habitats. This has allowed to captured some wonderful close-up and wider in habitat images. I rarely use additional light, but when I do I prefer a soft, constant light over a flash and only apply the light as I take the shot, removing it immediately afterwards.

Why Forgotten Little Creatures?

The idea for the Forgotten Little Creatures project and this book came from a general lack of positive coverage of smaller species we have close to Frome, in Somerset. The project has developed over the years and this book is the culmination of over four years of work recording and photographing plants, invertebrates, amphibians and reptiles within a 40 mile radius of my home in Frome. Within this boundary I am very lucky to have Cley Hill, the Mendip Hills, the Polden Hills, Somerset Levels and a very special reserve in Wiltshire.

The project is a celebration of these forgotten little creatures, using artistic imagery and interesting science facts to illustrate the beauty, characters and charm of these smaller, less-loved and often overlooked species. This book is a selection of just some of the incredible species found at the locations mentioned above and also ones I have found even in my own garden, showing how even a small space can be important for wildlife. For each image I have included a short description along with the shooting details and any additional accessories I may have used. I have described the locations I have used but not given specific location details for the images, but with a little research you can find some wonderful areas local to you.

I hope that this collection of images, science facts and stories behind the images will inspire others to investigate the wildlife they have around them, and maybe to make a home for wildlife if they have the space, thereby giving the smaller species a little more love and appreciation; every species has an important role to play in maintaining healthy ecosystems, not just the more obvious mammals and the birds.

"It is that range of biodiversity that we must care for—the whole thing—rather than just one or two stars" - Sir David Attenborough.

Locations

All the images in this book were taken at just a handful of locations, three of which are within 30 miles of my home and one, Upper Waterhay, just under 40 miles away. Only the snake's head fritillary images were taken at this reserve. I have collected images over the last four years from these sites together with surveys of the numbers of each species found.

Mendip Hills

The Mendip Hills are comprised of a windswept plateau, flower rich limestone grasslands, caves, pools and ancient woodlands covering an area of 198 km². In 1972, the Mendips were designated as an Area of Outstanding Natural Beauty (ANOB) within which there are 7 naturally designated Geological Sites of Special Scientific Interest (SSSI) and 18 local Geological Sites. In terms of biodiversity there are 27 SSSIs, 3 Special Areas of Conservation (SAC), 1 Special Protection Area (SPA) and 2 National Nature Reserves.

The Mendip Hills were historically mined for lead and today numerous black slag piles containing high levels of lead, cadmium and zinc remain. These slag piles experience extremes of temperature, particularly in the summer months, as the black slag readily absorbs solar radiation. These particular areas are nutrient poor and only a small number of metal tolerant plants can grow in them. The area as a whole is home to nationally scarce species and important breeding sites for amphibians and reptiles.

Polden Hills and Cley Hill

Both the Polden Hills and Cley Hill (facing page) are calcareous grasslands, an intricate and diverse ecosystem containing many specialist species that are found nowhere else. These chalk grasslands are in decline due to changes in farming; in some cases, reduced grazing leads to the dominance of coarse grasses, scrub and woodland. For some sites, huge increases in recreational use have resulted in compacted soil and trampled vegetation. The Polden Hills are home to several nationally scarce species including the Large Blue Butterfly and Rufous Grasshopper. Cley Hill is designated as an SSSI with both geological and archaeological importance.

Somerset Levels

The Somerset Levels and Moors are the UK's largest wetland areas, nestled between the Blackdown Hills and the Mendip Hills and bisected by the Polden Hills. The area covers over 650 km², within which are 32 SSSIs, 12 SPAs and over 10 nature reserves. The Somerset Levels and Moors have long been used for food and fuel, and the area is now a big draw for tourists and wildlife enthusiasts year round. The traditionally managed habitats contain a rich biodiversity that is both nationally and internationally important. The area, which adjoins agricultural fields and pastures, is managed by several different organisations that work closely together. Although probably best known for birds—with huge flocks of starlings in the winter, as well as breeding bitterns and great white egrets—it is also an important area for many wildflower, invertebrate, amphibian and reptile species.

Upper Waterhay

Upper Waterhay is a small meadow surrounded by farmland. It was purchased in 1970 by Wiltshire Wildlife Trust as it is one of only a handful of strongholds left for the rare snake's head fritillary. The trust now manage this meadow for these rare flowers and it is still grazed by cattle over winter.

Plants

Plants are the life support system of ecosystems and every food chain in nature starts with plants. They are some of the only organisms that are able to convert energy from the sun into food and in turn provide, directly or indirectly, all the food that we eat. In addition to providing food, they absorb carbon dioxide and release vital oxygen into the atmosphere. Approximately 25% of medications prescribed today originated from wild plants and many people also rely on herbal medicines for their health and well-being.

In addition to holding onto rain water and capturing carbon, wildflower meadows can be biodiversity hotspots and are important habitats and food sources for invertebrates that also pollinate our food crops.

Looking beyond the ecological importance of plants and wildflowers, the green spaces within urban environments can help to reduce both air and noise pollution, helping to promote healthier living and increased well-being by encouraging more active lifestyles and by reducing stress. There is something so beautiful about seeing wildflowers growing along roadsides, in fields and in our gardens, and walking through a wildflower meadow is a wonderful experience for all the senses. Amongst the more typically beautiful plants, there are also the semi-parasitic and carnivorous plants, not necessarily beautiful by average standards, but in every way fascinating and curious subjects of study.

Springtime is a wonderful time of new growth and colour and there is nothing more iconic of spring in the United Kingdom than Bluebells. Carpets of these beautiful flowers form in our ancient woodlands. These wildflowers are slow growing, taking between five and seven years to grow from a seed to a bulb capable of flowering, so the magnificent carpets we see in some woodlands have taken many, many years to develop. The bulbs themselves are actually poisonous, containing biologically active compounds that help protect them from insect and larger animal pests.

The name for British Bluebells, *Hyacinthoides non-scripta*, is believed to have originated from a Greek myth. 'Non-scripta' means unlettered or unmarked, and was used to distinguish the bluebells from the hyacinths that grew from the blood of Prince Hyacinthus, on the petals of which Apollo wrote the word 'alas' as a lament to the young prince.

There is so much more to bluebells than the beautiful flowers we see in springtime. In Medieval times, it was believed that the bluebell rang out to summon fairies, but any human that heard the ring would soon die. During the Bronze Age, a sticky sap produced in the bulb was used to glue feathers to arrows and later the same sticky substance was also used in book binding.

Bluebells and Spider's Webs

In the woodlands behind my house is a steep bank that in springtime is a blanket of bluebells. As the sun rises high enough, the most wonderful light penetrates the trees to the woodland floor. Those first rays of light illuminate the water droplets and spider webs, producing some great textures, patterns and colours. I found this smaller bluebell slightly on its own and the way the light played on the spiders web really caught my eye, I used a wide aperture to just start to bring the web into focus but not so much that it would detract from the bluebell.

Wild British Bluebells (*Hyacinthoides non-scripta*)
Canon 5D Mark III with Sigma 180mm f/2.8 macro lens
Aperture f/3.5 | ISO 200 | Shutter speed 1/320sec

Bluebells are protected in the UK under the Wildlife and Countryside Act (1981), which prevents them from being illegally dug up from the countryside or removed from land for sale; they were also listed on Schedule 8 of the Act in 1998, making the trade in wild bluebell bulbs or seeds illegal unless you have a license. Despite this, a lack of understanding of their delicate nature is putting the magnificent bluebell carpets at risk as their popularity as a photographic subject increases. The drive to capture something different or even a pet or family photo in amongst the bluebells is causing potentially irreversible damage.

When the leaves are trampled they die back and are unable to photosynthesise, depleting food supplies for the following year and reducing their ability to flower. If no further damage is caused they can take years to regenerate. In some of the more popular spots the damage can be significant and repeated trampling results in the flowers being unable to produce seeds, and in some places this has led to woodland paths widening as those plants closest to the path die back. In the last couple of years, fences have been installed in some places to protect the bluebells by preventing anyone from walking through them.

Bluebell Woodland Painting
An image of the local bluebell woodland using intentional camera movement (ICM) to give a painted feel to the image as the blues and greens of the bluebell plants combine with the grey/browns of the beech trees.

Wild British Bluebells (*Hyacinthoides non-scripta*)
Canon 5D Mark III with Canon 100mm f/2.8 macro lens
Aperture f/22 | ISO 50 | Shutter speed 0.6sec

Our native bluebells are also under threat from hybridisation with non-native Spanish bluebells that are often planted in gardens. If you want to plant bluebells, there are places where you can purchase our native British bluebells rather than the Spanish species. Beautiful as bluebells are, however, they are best seen in their natural habitat and, with a little thought and common sense, the wonderful carpets of bluebells that signify spring for so many can be preserved for future generations to enjoy.

Shades of Grey

Photographing through the flowers and using them to frame a specific flower stalk can produce some interesting patterns. To further enhance the patterns on this image, I have converted it to black and white. You rarely see black and white images of bluebells, which is understandable as their colour is just so stunning, but when you remove that colour you begin to notice more details including the patterns they create.

I experimented with apertures for this shot until I achieved the effect I was looking for. It's important to take your time with all your photography as this really focuses your mind on the different images you could achieve and allows you to start seeing different possibilities.

Wild British Bluebells (*Hyacinthoides non-scripta*)
Canon 5D Mark III with Canon 100mm f/2.8 macro lens
Aperture f/5.6 | ISO 500 | Shutter speed 1/60sec

Snake's head Fritillary

Wet meadows of snake's head fritillaries were once a common sight and the flowers were so abundant that they were collected and sold in the markets of London. Over the years, the combination of meadow drainage and conversion of land for farming has meant that these beautiful wild flowers survive in only a handful of protected sites.

Crimson

The normal colour for snake's head fritillaries is a beautiful deep red or crimson, and these really stand out in the meadows against the grass and creamy white variants. As the sun rises above the trees and starts to light up the meadows, these crimson flowers almost glow in that early morning light like mini beacons. To achieve this shot I lay carefully in the grass to avoid flattening any neighbouring flowers and, using a wide aperture, composed the shot with the flower to one side, focusing just on the flower itself and allowing the textures of the grass and the light playing on the grasses to create the backdrop.

Wild Snake's head Fritillary (*Fritillaria meleagris*)
Canon 5D Mark III with Sigma 180mm f/2.8 macro lens
Aperture f/2.8 | ISO 200 | Shutter speed 1/800sec

A couple of these sites are found in Wiltshire where they are carefully managed by Wiltshire Wildlife Trust. At one of these sites, uniquely, two thirds of the population are creamy white rather than normal crimson colour.

Flowering starts around mid-April and lasts for just a few weeks; if you visit when the conditions are just right, the meadows are covered in a blanket of dew that sparkles in the early morning sun.

Snake's Heads and Rainbows

Watching the weather forecast carefully for several days, I waited until the conditions looked perfect for dew formation and, on arrival at the site, there was not only a thick blanket of dew but also mist. As the sun rose, the mist started to burn off resulting in a sparkling blanket of dew in amongst which were these two beautiful, creamy white fritillaries. I used a small LED light hidden in the grass to light the flowers from below and shot at ground level through the grass. It wasn't until I looked at the image afterwards that I realised I had managed to capture a mini rainbow underneath the flowers.

Wild Snake's head Fritillary (*Fritillaria meleagris*)
Canon 5D Mark III with Sigma 180mm f/2.8 macro lens, Manfrotto Lumimuse 6 with diffusers
Aperture f/2.8 | ISO 160 | Shutter speed 1/2500sec

The Lone Flower

Finding a single flower on its own, I wanted to show the delicateness of the flower blending into the dew covered grass by shooting from ground level through the grass behind the flower, as the position of the flower in relation to the sun enhanced the bokeh of the light on the dew. The flower is lit from beneath using an LED light with diffusers just to add some subtle illumination.

Wild Snake's head Fritillary (*Fritillaria meleagris*)
Canon 5D Mark III with Sigma 180mm f/2.8 macro lens, Manfrotto Lumimuse 6 with diffusers
Aperture f/5 | ISO 160 | Shutter speed 1/800sec

Snowdrops are the first flower we see in the year, appearing from January onwards with flowering peaking around late February to March depending on the weather. Once thought to be native to the UK, it is now thought to have been introduced to the islands by the Romans. It was first recorded growing wild in the late 18th Century and is now widely naturalised, creating beautiful white carpets in the first few months of the year. The wild snowdrops we seen in our woodlands are *Galanthus nivalis* meaning "milk flower of the snow" (*Galanthus* comes from the Greek *Gala* "milk", *anthos* "flower" and nivalis meaning "from the snow") and the word snowdrop is believed to have come from the earrings that women wore in the 15th to 17th centuries.

Woodland Snowdrops

In the wooded valley behind my house there is a small area next to the river where, each year, the snowdrops appear amongst the fallen branches and stinging nettles which seem to start appearing around the same time the snowdrops are in full flower. This makes obtaining a low perspective of these plants rather interesting, and after a while one is more or less forced to accept that being stung numerous times by nettles is inevitable. However, when everything comes together it is worth the discomfort, and the pain usually wears off after a few hours.

For this image I wanted to find a way to incorporate the habitat and found this small clump growing around a fallen branch, the colours and texture of which fitted perfectly with the colours and light in the whole image.

Snowdrops (*Galanthus nivalis*)
Canon 7D with Canon 100mm f/2.8 macro lens
Aperture f/3.5 | ISO 200 | Shutter speed 1/320sec

Snowdrops are fascinating little plants and actually contain antifreeze proteins that inhibit the formation of ice crystals, preventing them from freezing in cold spells. As spring temperatures reach 10 ºC, the petals open to reveal the pollen and nectar, which are vital—if not the only—sources of food for early emerging bumblebees. Snowdrop bulbs are actually poisonous to humans and can cause nausea, vomiting and diarrhoea if eaten in significant quantities.

Despite being a naturalised introduced species that can be seen in huge carpets, the Snowdrop is actually listed as Near Threatened on the IUCN Redlist due to habitat destruction and collection for the horticultural trade. The species is under threat in some countries where they are native, and all snowdrop species are listed in CITES Appendix II.

Afternoon Light
For a short while on sunny days the afternoon sun comes through the trees and lights up the dead bracken, giving it an interesting peachy-orange glow. This image was taken at 4pm on a beautiful February afternoon when the snowdrops were in full flower. By lying on the ground and shooting through some of the foliage I was able to focus on this unopened snowdrop using the larger snowdrops in the background to frame it against the peachy backdrop.

Snowdrops (*Galanthus nivalis*)
Canon 5D Mark III with Sigma 180mm f/2.8 macro lens
Aperture f/4 | ISO 250 | Shutter speed 1/200sec

Anemones and Rainbows

Wood anemones tend to appear around the same time as the bluebells and you can often find beautiful congregations of the two growing together in ancient woodlands where the white of the wood anemone contrasts beautifully with the bluish purple of the bluebells.

Wood anemones are incredibly slow growers which makes them great indicators of ancient woodlands; they rely on the growth of their root system to spread, rather than the dissemination of seeds, and can take up to 100 years to spread just six feet. These beautiful white flowers get their name from the Greek *Anemone* meaning "daughter of the wind" with one of the old common names for the flower being windflower; the name *nemorosa* is from the Latin *nemus* meaning forest, a reference to where they grow. They are actually poisonous, containing protoanemonin, which can cause skin irritation and illness if ingested.

I only recently discovered this area of anemones and bluebells growing in a wooded valley behind my house; overnight this area becomes very damp, resulting in a covering of dew in the morning and the most wonderful light as the sun comes through the trees. This image was actually an accident; I hadn't realised I had so many water drops on the end of my lens and as the sun hit the lens the water reflected, refracted and dispersed the light creating the rainbows. I shot through the foliage to soften the overall image using a wide aperture to keep the focus on the anemone flower.

Wood Anemone (*Anemone nemorosa*)
Canon 5D Mark III with Sigma 180mm f/2.8 macro lens
Aperture f/2.8 | ISO 320 | Shutter speed 1/400sec

Feeling Blue

Chalk milkwort is a small, perennial herb to 5 cm tall typically found on closely grazed chalk grasslands. Although it can be locally abundant, it has disappeared from some localities due to habitat loss, as well as lack of grazing, which allows coarser grasses to become dominant.

These beautiful little blue flowers adorn the slopes of the chalk grassland and, being small, allow you to rest the camera right on the ground to shoot through the grasses and create a soft green bokeh around the plant making the blue really stand out; this is further enhanced by using a wide aperture.

Chalk Milkwort (*Polygala calcarea*)
Canon 5D Mark III with Canon 100mm f/2.8 macro lens
Aperture f/2.8 | ISO 200 | Shutter speed 1/640sec

The Humble Daisy

Possibly one of the most overlooked flowers when it comes to photography is the daisy, which grows in lawns everywhere and provides a food source for many different invertebrates. There are over 4000 species of daisy and they are found worldwide with the exception of Antarctica. Daisies open and close each day with the daylight and this is where they are thought to get their name from; "daes eage" is an old English term meaning "day's eye".

Interestingly the daisy is technically two types of flower in one; the white petals are one flower and the yellow florets are another. As children we would make daisy chains to give to one another in the summer. These beautiful little flowers are rarely photographed, being often ignored for rarer or more elaborate flowers, but spend an hour or so with them and their fine qualities become very apparent. This image is of a daisy growing on the front lawn, shot from slightly underneath to illustrate the pink colour to the underside of their petals, using the sky as a clear background.

Common Daisy (*Bellis perennis*)
Canon 5D Mark III with Canon 100mm f/2.8 macro lens
Aperture f/5.6 | ISO 160 | Shutter speed 1/250sec

Carpet of Eyebright

Eyebrights are taxonomically tricky to tell apart; there are around 20 species and these easily hybridise, giving rise to many hybrids. The common name 'eyebright' refers to its use as a treatment for eye infections. These little plants are semi-parasitic, feeding off the nutrients in the roots of other plants including grasses. August is a lovely time to photograph these plants as they are often covered in dew first thing in the morning and sparkle in the early morning light. These pair of flower stalks were sticking out much higher from the surrounding vegetation, allowing me to compose the shot with them to one side, using the other flowers to create colours in the out of focus background.

Eyebright (*Euphrasia*)
Canon 5D Mark III with Canon 100mm f/2.8 macro lens
Aperture f/2.8 | ISO 400 | Shutter speed 1/6400sec

Painted Parsley

Cow parsley is a common sight along road verges, the edges of woodlands, grasslands, farmland and hedges. At times it seems to be taking over, crowding out other wildflowers entirely in some spots. Many of our wildflowers actually rely on nutrient poor soil to thrive, but an increase in fertilisers used on farmland, the addition of nitrogen oxides from vehicle exhausts and changes in the way verges are managed—they used to be grazed but are now cut, with the cuttings left to add further nutrients—has lead to nutrient rich soils allowing larger plants like cow parsley to flourish. That said, its beautifully delicate flowers are an important food source for many invertebrate species and at the edges of woodlands the dappled light coming through the trees creates a dreamlike scene. It is that dreamlike atmosphere contrasted against the tangled cow parsley flower heads that I wanted to capture here, using a wide aperture and the light coming through the trees to bring detail to the background.

Cow Parsley (*Anthriscus sylvestris*)
Canon 5D Mark III with Sigma 180mm f/2.8 macro lens
Aperture f/2.8 | ISO 200 | Shutter speed 1/500sec

Yellow and Purple

Heather and gorse are fundamental parts of many habitats, providing both shelter and food for a great number of different species from insects to adders. When both plants are in flower the contrast in colours can be striking. In September they both flower at the same time, bringing a beautiful blanket of colour to large parts of some of the Mendips. It was this colour I wanted to capture in this image. I used a wide aperture to give a shallow depth of field, focusing on the gorse flower with the heather flowers providing the framing.

Heather (*Calluna vulgaris*) and Western Gorse (*Ulex galli*)
Canon 5D Mark III with Canon 100mm f/2.8 macro lens
Aperture f/2.8 | ISO 125 | Shutter speed 1/1250sec

Beautiful but Deadly—to an Insect

The round leaved sundew is one of two native carnivorous plants found at this nature reserve (the other being the intermediate sundew). In the summer they can form carpets at a few spots. These fascinating little plants wait for unsuspecting insects to be attracted to the glistening, adhesive droplets on their leaves. Once stuck to a leaf, the leaf curls up and secreted digestive enzymes break down the insect, allowing the nutrients, which other plants usually sequester from the soil, to be absorbed by the plant. As inhabitants of very nutrient poor habitats, this mechanism allows them to thrive where other plants cannot.

They are not easy plants to photograph on account of their small size, but with a little experimentation the ideas start to come. One thing that really caught my eye was the way the crimson tentacles and sticky secretions glistened in the August sun. Finding myself a location that would allow me to lie on the ground I was able to shoot through mosses and adjacent sundews using a wide aperture to soften the whole image.

Round-leaved Sundew (*Drosera rotundifolia*)
Canon 5D Mark III with Sigma 180mm f/2.8 macro lens
Aperture f/3.5 | ISO 250 | Shutter speed 1/1250sec

Perfect Roosting Sites

The tall grasses and brackens that are abundant across many reserves are some of the best places to find invertebrates, especially damselflies, making them a great place to start your search.

It was whilst looking for invertebrates that I actually noticed just how beautiful these plants are in their own right, especially when covered in dew and glistening in the early morning light.

In late May the bracken fronds are still unfurling, which adds textures and details to any image; to capture this particular image I shot through the grasses, picking out one particular bracken stem to focus on. I used an aperture that would bring enough detail to the whole image without becoming distracting. As you can see, it was a very heavy dew that morning and I got very, very wet capturing this image!

Grasses and Bracken (*Pteridium aquilinum*)
Canon 5D Mark III with Sigma 180mm f/2.8 macro lens
Aperture f/5.6 | ISO 400 | Shutter speed 1/1000sec

Small White Flowers of Spring

Common whitlow grass flowers from March onwards on the Mendips. These plants produce tiny but beautiful little white flowers that grow on many of the rocky areas, often in amongst mosses. The flower stalks are no more than 10 cm tall, so they can easily be missed. To capture the diminutive size and beauty of these flowers, they need to be photographed from ground level. By lying prostrate and resting my camera on the ground, I was able to capture these little flowers sticking up above the surrounding vegetation on the rocks.

Common Whitlowgrass (*Erophila verna*)
Canon 5D Mark III with Canon 100mm f/2.8 macro lens
Aperture f/2.8 | ISO 320 | Shutter speed 1/2500sec

Orchids

Orchids (Orchidaceae) are one the largest and most diverse families of flowering plants with over 25,000 described species. They are one of the oldest flower groups in existence and are subjects of great fascination and even mania amongst their admirers. Why this is so is not certain, but they have become amongst the most widely cultivated of all horticultural subjects.

Here in the United Kingdom we have between 50 and 60 orchid species. Of these, several types favour the same sorts of habitats, and this is especially true of the calcicolous species, which inhabit the chalk grasslands I have surveyed and photographed at locally.

There is something about orchids that vies for attention beyond that of other wildflowers, with many people travelling long distances and at great expense just to see certain species. Unfortunately I have seen first-hand the damage that can be caused to both the flowers and the surrounding habitat when people are not careful. Despite all our wild orchids being protected under section 13 of the Wildlife and Countryside Act (1981), there are still those who dig them up to take home, either to try to cultivate them or to sell them for profit. This is one of the reasons that the sites of some of our rarest orchids are now closely guarded secrets.

A Rare Beauty

If you look closely it is amazing what you can find. This beautiful but rare natural hybrid of the bee orchid and fly orchid is found in only a handful of locations in the UK. Given how small both parent plants are, is it surprising just how tall this hybrid is. I found this flower in amongst the ox-eye daisies. I used the gap in the hedge behind the flowers to make them stand, while the surrounding plants served to frame the rare and beautiful subjects, a wide aperture serving to soften everything but the one flower. I used an aperture that would allow enough detail to come into the background without becoming too distracting.

Bee Orchid x Fly Orchid (*Ophrys apifera* × *Ophrys insectifera*)
Canon 5D Mark III with Sigma 180mm f/2.8 macro lens
Aperture f/4 | ISO 400 | Shutter speed 1/800sec

Painted Orchid

Common spotted orchids are, as the name suggests, one of our more common orchids and plants can be found on grass verges, roadsides (if left uncut) and meadows in more pristine areas.

These orchids can vary in colour from deep purple through to pink and white. The name comes from the spots on the petals, but even so you can occasionally find some that have no markings at all, these usually having white petals.

They really are stunning flowers and, along with bee orchids, are probably one of the most photographed orchids in this area, so it can be tricky to find an original angle. They have beautiful colours, textures and patterns, which is where I got my inspiration for this image; by going in close and photographing through the flowers instead of focusing on the flowers, I achieved a softer and more painted effect for this image, capturing something a little bit different.

Common Spotted Orchid (*Dactylorhiza fuchsii*)
Canon 5D Mark III with Sigma 180mm f/2.8 macro lens
Aperture f/3.2 | ISO 400 | Shutter speed 1/320sec

Against The Sky

Greater butterfly orchids are tall, stunning orchids that favour chalk grasslands. That said, they are not found on all chalk grasslands. They are quite distinctive, with their white flowers which can number up to 40 on a spike, standing out from the grasses and other orchids and emitting a fine vanilla scent that grows stronger towards the evening to attract pollinating moths. Like most orchids, their petals have incredible textures that become apparent only when viewed closely. This can be hard to capture, but being quite tall, it is sometimes possible to carefully position oneself underneath them and photograph them looking upwards as I have done here, using the blue sky as the backdrop.

By shooting at this angle I have used the sunlight to pick out the textures and was also able to use an aperture of f/10 without having to worry out bringing distracting details into the background. The white and pale green are really set off by the blue of the sky.

Greater Butterfly Orchid (*Platanthera chlorantha*)
Canon 5D Mark III with Canon 100mm f/2.8 macro lens
Aperture f/10 | ISO 320 | Shutter speed 1/800sec

From the Grass

The bee orchid is an unmistakable flower found on grasslands and frequently in disused quarries. The name comes from its mimicry of its main pollinator, a type of bee, which is thought to have driven the evolution of the flower itself. You can easily imagine how, as inspection of the flowers shows that they do resemble a bee resting on a pink flower.

That said, the species of bee it mimics doesn't actually occur in the UK, so our populations of bee orchid have evolved to self-pollinate. In some years there can be large numbers of bee orchids, while in others few if any plants are apparent. This is because the seedlings take up to six years to flower and, though they do perennate, plants may only flower a handful of times in their lifespan.

These are probably one of the most photogenic orchids and finding a new angle or something a little more creative to get viewers thinking can be tricky. I came across this small bee orchid whilst out walking and noticed it as I looked at it from above, giving me the inspiration for this image. Using a wide aperture and shooting almost down onto it, I was able to give the impression of it growing out of the grass, its vibrant colours really standing out against the green.

Bee Orchid (*Ophrys apifera*)
Canon 5D Mark III with Canon 100mm f/2.8 macro lens
Aperture f/3.2 | ISO 400 | Shutter speed 1/2000sec

Invertebrates

Invertebrates are not only incredibly important to the survival of ecosystems as a whole they are also incredibly interesting with fascinating life cycles, wing and eye structures and have just as much character as birds and mammals. Invertebrates make up 97% of all animal species on Earth with over 1.3million species described so far and although most are small their role in ecosystems is vital. They are important pollinators and that's not just bees; many different species help to pollinate food crops for other animals and of course for us humans. They provide a food source for other invertebrates, fish, birds, mammals, specialised plants and even humans, and some are important natural pest controllers with only a small percentage actually considered as pests. There are some species that help to clear and clean up habitats by eating decaying matter, faeces and leaf litter and they help to maintain soil quality which in turn aids agriculture and also helps out in our gardens. To put it another way, we simply cannot live without them and once you start looking closely at these animals you will notice just how wonderful they really are.

"If we and the rest of the back-boned animals were to disappear overnight, the rest of the world would get on pretty well. But if invertebrates were to disappear, the world's ecosystems would collapse" - Sir David Attenborough

The Grasshopper and the Dragon Fly
Very occasionally you can be photographing one species when another completely different one appears. Whilst photographing this female black tailed skimmer dragonfly in the early morning light, a little grasshopper nymph appeared from low down in the grass. It's not often that you have the chance to capture two different species in the same image, so it's always worth keeping a close eye on what is happening around you.

Black-tailed Skimmer (*Orthetrum cancellatum*) and Grasshopper Nymph
Canon 5D Mark III with Sigma 180mm f/2.8 macro lens
Aperture f/4.5 | ISO 400 | Shutter speed 1/800sec

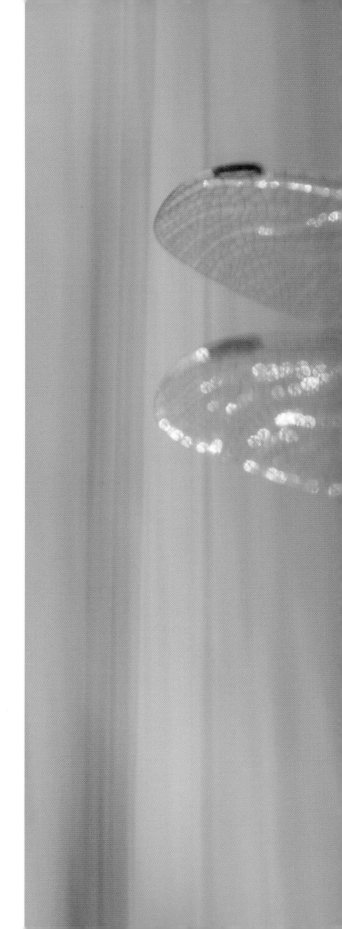

Butterflies and Moths

Butterflies and moths belong to the order Lepidoptera which, in Greek, means 'scale wing'. Their wings are covered in thousands of scales consisting of tiny overlapping pieces of chitin. It is these scales that produce the wing patterns and colours we see and, in males, release pheromones that attract females. There are actually three types of scales;

- The pigmentary scales contain coloured compounds that are sequestered from larval food plants. It is the juxtaposition and amount of pigment in each scale that creates the illusion of different colours.
- The larger structural scales are semi-transparent and some of them have a microscopic prismatic structure that refracts the light, giving rise to the iridescence seen in some species. It the mixture of pigmentary and structural scales that gives rise to the wide range of colours we see. In addition, these scales contain an ultraviolet pattern that is visible to other butterflies which is vital for finding and attracting mates.
- The androconia scales are mainly found on the forewings of males. At the base of these are tiny, pheromone-containing sacs that are used to entice females to copulate.

Butterflies and moths are a flagship invertebrate group and most people feel affection for them, with thousands of people monitoring them every year and many more planting their gardens specifically to attract them. Moreover they are important indicators of a healthy ecosystem with areas rich in butterflies and moths tending to be rich in other invertebrate species. Not only are they important pollinators, especially of wild flowers, but they also provide a vital food source for a range of insectivorous species including other invertebrates, birds and mammals.

The life cycle of Lepidopterans from egg to caterpillar to chrysalis to butterfly is truly one of the wonders of nature.

Orange-Tip Camouflage

Female orange-tip butterfly well camouflaged against the green leaves, she was so well camouflaged I spent several minutes trying to point her out to some interested people. If you have the chance to look closely at the incredible, mottled camouflage colouration of the underwings of the orange-tip butterfly you will discover a finely balanced mixture of yellow and black scales. On finding this female I set about looking for a different angle to photograph her from and decided on trying to shoot from below her eye level which meant getting very wet crouching down in the dew covered grass. By shooting from such a low angle I was able to capture her wonderful eye peeking through the leaves.

Orange-Tip Butterfly (*Anthocharis cardamines*)
Canon 5D Mark III with Sigma 180mm f/2.8 macro lens
Aperture f/6.3 | ISO 320 | Shutter speed 1/160sec

Marbled White Butterflies

Marbled white butterflies (*Melangaria galathea*) despite what the name suggests actually belong to the brown butterflies (Satyrinae) and the English names for them come from ancient terms meaning marbling "Marmoris" (Benjamin Wilkes and 18th century artist and naturalist) and "The Marmoress" by Moses Harris (18th century English entomologist).

These are one of our most striking butterflies with an interesting background to the variations in the creamy/white colouration in the wings. Angela Wilson discovered the tint of this paler area is dependent on the caterpillars' ability to break down two different flavonoid chemicals found in the grasses they eat, in particular red fescue. There are several derivations of these flavonoid that are stored in the body and deposited after pupation into the paler areas of the wings; the higher the concentration of the flavonoids, the more yellow the wings.

Moonlight Silhouette

Visiting grasslands at dawn or dusk during their short flight period you can observe the incredible marbled markings as they roost. Early morning after a chilly night sees them covered in dew but visiting in the evenings can reward you with incredible evening light and if you time it just right a full moon. Moonlight silhouette was taken as the full moon appeared from behind a bank of trees providing the perfect backdrop to the roosting marbled white butterfly.

Marbled white butterfly (*Melangaria galathea*)
Canon 5D Mark III with Sigma 180mm f/2.8 macro lens, Gitzo tripod and head.
Aperture f/4 | ISO 1000 | Shutter speed 1/80sec

Patterns

The wings of the marbled white are striking and it is easy to see where the ancient names meaning marbling came from, especially when seen in black and white. As the weeks pass the butterflies start to show wear and tear in their wings and where scales have been rubbed off their wings become more translucent and in the case of the marble white show of that marbling beautifully. To achieve this image I found a butterfly that was warming up quite high in the grasses allowing me to get underneath it and shoot upwards using the sky as the clear backdrop. Shooting into the sky produces challenges and in this situation the face of the butterfly was in complete shadow so I used a small LED light, on a low setting and diffused to add some fill in light.

Marbled white butterfly (*Melangaria galathea*)
Canon 5D Mark III with Canon 100mm f/2.8 macro lens, Gitzo tripod and head, Manfrotto Lumimuse 6 with diffusers.
Aperture f/11 | ISO 400 | Shutter speed 1/250sec

Green hairstreaks are small butterflies with wingspans of less than 35 mm. They are some of the first butterflies to emerge in the early spring, with an incredible metallic green produced on the underside of the wings, in stark contrast to the brown of the upper wings. They are relatively easy butterflies to photograph if you can find them amongst the foliage as they perch with their wings closed and the green colour showing. Once you do find them they are not a flighty butterfly, spending the majority of their time perched within their territory.

The eyes of butterflies, as with many invertebrates, are made up of thousands of individual light receptors each with their own microscopic lenses (ommatidia) through which they are able to see a mosaic of the habitat around them. These compound eyes allow them to perceive visible radiation but also make them sensitive to UV patterns on plants which they use to locate specific plants. They are also capable of detecting polarised light to determine the position of the sun; if you watch them as they warm up in the morning, you can see them moving in relation to the position of the sun.

Wrapped Up

Males are highly territorial spending large proportions of their time perched at the edges of their territories ready to chase away rival males, other butterflies and any other flying invertebrates. At this site the main area for the green hairstreaks is a large patch of gorse and hawthorn high up on the hillside, but I came across this male lower down perched on a partially curled hawthorn leaf. This was a tricky image to capture as the butterfly and leaf are backlit by the sun and you can see the silhouette of the rest of the butterfly in the leaf, but with some perseverance, a little bit of high cloud cover I managed to get there in the end!

Green Hairstreak (*Callophrys rubi*)
Canon 5D Mark III with Canon 100mm f/2.8 macro lens
Aperture f/6.3 | ISO 250 | Shutter speed 1/125sec

Full Frontal

A male perched amongst the hawthorn higher up on the hillside. This individual was shot face-on, showing how difficult they can be to spot initially, the bright green metallic colour of the underwings blending in well with the new growth of the hawthorn leaves. If you sit still and watch a while you can see them moving their heads ever so slightly as they observe the area around them. They really are quite adorable when seen head-on with those dark eyes looking right back at you.

Green Hairstreak (*Callophrys rubi*)
Canon 5D Mark III with Canon 100mm f/2.8 macro lens
Aperture f/5 | ISO 500 | Shutter speed 1/400sec

During the last few days before the adult emerges, different genes are switched on and off to regulate the colours and patterns of both the upper and underwings. Every now and then, changes in environmental conditions can cause colour variations in the wings known as aberrations. Extremes of temperature while the butterfly is developing in the chrysalis alter the way the colour compounds are transferred to the scales and large temperature variations may result in dramatic changes in colouration.

Aberration

Historically and to some extent this continues today, chalkhill blue aberrations were some of the most sort after butterflies at the heyday of British butterfly collecting with some sites experiencing large numbers of people all trying to net certain aberrations. Today there are still a great number of people that search out these aberrations, of which there are 87 named, but instead of trying catch them they try to photograph them for their collection which is much preferred and I have met a couple of these photographic aberration hunters when I've been out on the reserves. I haven't found many aberrations at this particular site however, in August 2015, daytime temperatures at one site were routinely in the mid-twenties, but during the night temperatures plummeted to just a few degrees above zero resulting in a couple of aberrations; this is one that I came across. It lacks much of the dark colouration of the normal adults.

Chalkhill Blue Butterfly (Polyommatus coridon)
Canon 5D Mark III with Canon 100mm f/2.8 macro lens
Aperture f/4.5 | ISO 640 | Shutter speed 1/200sec

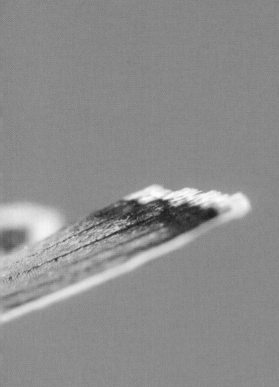

Ready For Take-Off

Once the sun is up, the butterflies open their wings angling them to the direction of the sun to absorb the warmth ready to take to the air in search of food and a mate, at this point they don't hang around for long especially on hot days. I was lucky to find this male with his wings open perched on a seed head in a position that if I laid on the ground I would be able to capture him head on against the clear blue sky. Moments after taking this shot he took to the wing.

Chalkhill Blue Butterfly (Polyommatus coridon)
Canon 5D Mark III with Canon 100mm f/2.8 macro lens
Aperture f/7.1 | ISO 500 | Shutter speed 1/1000sec

Blending In

The colours of the wings of the common blues are produced in a combination of ways to produce the striking blue we see. Tyndall Scattering is partly responsible for the blue we see and occurs as light is scattered by multiple layers of three-dimensional diffraction gratings in the chitin, this same effect is responsible for the blue eyes in humans and the blue sky we see. In addition to this scattering effect, the blue colour is further enhanced by the pigments in the scales which are synthesised during scale development just days before the adult butterfly emerges and then added to this some of the colours is a result of flavonoids obtained by the caterpillars from the vetches they eat.

Early in the morning when you will find these butterflies with their wings closed showing the markings on the underside of their wings and it's surprising how well they are camouflaged in the long grasses. Instead of taking a close-up shot, I decided to take a step back and show her in her habitat and it is such a crucial part to their survival. I used a wide aperture to blur out the background but keeping enough detail to create a patterned backdrop.

Common Blue Butterfly (*Polyommatus icarus*)
Canon 5D Mark III with Canon 100mm f/2.8 macro lens
Aperture f/2.8 | ISO 320 | Shutter speed 1/4000sec

Small skippers are beautiful golden butterflies found on tall, rough grassland and depending on the weather start emerging anytime from mid-June onwards. The "Streakt Cloudy Hog" was an early name given to small skippers by Petiver in 1704, but this largely disappeared with the publication of *The Aurelian or natural history of insects* by Moses Harris in 1766.

I think these are one of the most adorable butterflies you can find with the cutest of faces and they can be relatively easy to photograph, especially the females as they are much more sedentary perching for long periods. I'm very lucky that one of the sites I survey has good populations of numerous different butterfly species. Over the years, I have come to know the best spots to locate each species.

Morning Warm Up

As well as taking close up shots of butterflies I do think it's important to take a step back once in a while and show the butterfly in its habitat and this is something I'm doing more and more as the relationship between butterflies and their habitats is fundamental to the survival of both. It can be tricky shooting in habitat shots as quite often they are very busy and congested grasslands and over the last year or so pretty breezy too. Having found this individual I set up the tripod and manually focused to the area I knew the butterfly would be once the breeze died down and waited. I opted for a wide aperture focusing purely on the butterfly allowing my background to be thrown out whilst keeping the wonderful colours and some textures.

Small Skipper (*Thymelicus sylvestris*)
Canon 5D Mark III with Sigma 180mm f/2.8 macro lens, Gitzo tripod and head.
Aperture f/3.2 | ISO 400 | Shutter speed 1/1600sec

Head Shot

I think the small skipper would win the award for most adorable butterfly, they have the most delightful faces when seen head on and certainly have a fluffy appearance especially when they first start to appear.

Small Skipper (*Thymelicus sylvestris*)
Canon 5D Mark III with Sigma 180mm f/2.8 macro lens, Gitzo tripod and head.
Aperture f/5.6 | ISO 500 | Shutter speed 1/200sec

Moths and butterflies both have compound eyes but the type of eye is actually different; nocturnal moths (and some butterflies) have superposition eyes, while diurnal or day flying moths (and most butterflies) have apposition eyes. Superposition eyes are adapted to low light conditions, producing much brighter images, whereas apposition eyes have better resolution and potential for colour vision.

Interestingly, the eyes of moths are covered in a natural coating of tiny protuberances that are smaller that the wavelength of incoming light. These reduce glare and improve their nocturnal vision. This natural coating has been mimicked in some types of anti-reflection coating that are used in our day to day lives, for example in glasses and camera lenses.

What Wind

Sometimes you have to take a chance on the weather conditions and just head out anyway as you may well be rewarded with some very comical results. The day I took this image was rather windy on the exposed grassland but that didn't deter the moths from feeding on the *Scabiosa*. I found this individual on the top of the flower battling the wind and, after numerous attempts to capture something in focus, I managed this shot of the moth at nearly a 90 degree angle to the flower, his the antennae blowing around in the wind with the focus on that incredible eye.

Brassy Longhorn Moth (*Nemophora metallica*)
Canon 5D Mark III with Canon 100mm f/2.8 macro lens
Aperture f/3.5 | ISO 400 | Shutter speed 1/1250sec

Moth wings are slightly different to those of butterflies and although moths are often thought of as being quite dull in colouration, the day flying moths can be quite brightly coloured. These bright colours are used as visual aids and to warn predators that they are poisonous.

Moth wings have a frenulum (a filament on the hindwing that couples with barbs on the forewing) which joins the wings together in flight; this structure is lacking in butterflies. The scales on the wings are slightly different too, with those of moths being larger giving some species a more furry appearance. Certainly, for the nocturnal species of moths these larger scales may help to conserve heat during the night and also aid in the absorption of the ultrasonic echolocation calls of bats.

Caught

The six-spot burnet moth is the commonest day flying moth in the UK, appearing from June onwards when it is often found feeding on blue or purple plants. The wings have striking red spots set against a dark, iridescent green background that is easily visible in sunlight. This colouration warns potential predators that these insects contain cyanide, obtained during the caterpillar stage as they feed on birdsfoot trefoil (*Lotus corniculatus*); this is carried through to the adult stage. Females can use plumes of this hydrogen cyanide combined with sexual pheromones to attract males.

In June you can often find them feeding on common spotted orchids; if you sit and watch them they can produce some wonderful moments, especially when they take a break from feeding and look right at where you're sitting. They can have such quizzical expressions sometimes and this is exactly what I wanted to capture in this photograph.

Six-Spot Burnet Moth (*Zygaena filipendulae*)
Canon 5D Mark III with Canon 100mm f/2.8 macro lens
Aperture f/5 | ISO 640 | Shutter speed 1/800sec

The antennae of some moths are very different to those of butterflies, as you can see in this image of a common forester moth, while some moths have antennae much longer than their bodies (as in the longhorned moths).

The antennae of both butterflies and moths are lined with receptors that are used to detect the scents of plants and the pheromones of mates, being thus essentially used for smell. The feathery antennae of moths are much more sensitive than those of butterflies and, through the use of mechanoreceptors, moths are able to detect tiny air currents as they fly through the air. This, combined with the scent receptors, helps with navigation at night.

Just Hanging Out

These moths can be quite hard to find as they are well camouflaged amongst the grass and only fly on bright, sunny days. If you find one and have a chance to look closely at the wings, you will observe that they are a stunning, metallic green colour. They also have feathered antennae, unlike the six-spot burnet moth with its clubbed antennae, even though they are of the same family (Zygaenids).

I found this individual on quite a dull day low down in the grass with its legs crossed and hooked over a leaf and those big dark eyes staring back at me. I used a small LED light to pick out its wonderful metallic appearance

Common Forester Moth (*Adscita statices*)
Canon 5D Mark III with Canon 100mm f/2.8 macro lens, Manfrotto Lumimuse 6
Aperture f/8 | ISO 400 | Shutter speed 1/100sec

Dragonflies and Damselflies

Dragonflies have existed on Earth for over 300 million years making them some of the first winged insects to have evolved and thus the most ancient. The oldest recognisable fossils belong to the Protodonata, considered to be the ancestors of dragonflies. Dragonflies belong to the order Odonata which comes from the Greek meaning 'toothed one', a reference to their serrated jaws.

There are over 5000 recognised species of Odonata. These are split into two suborders, the Anisoptera (true dragonflies), meaning 'unequal-winged', and the Zygoptera (damselflies) meaning 'even-winged'. Dragonflies are larger than damselflies and much stronger fliers. They are like mini helicopters when in flight whereas damselflies are much smaller, more delicate and weaker fliers. When roosting or at rest dragonflies hold their wings out from their bodies whereas those of damselflies are held along the length of the abdomen.

The majority of dragonflies and damselflies have bright metallic or iridescent colours produced by structural colours and pigment colours. The overall colouration we see is a combination of structural colours and yellow, red, brown and black pigments. Blue colours are created by the reflection of blue light off micro-structures in the cuticle, while green colours are created by the combination of a yellow pigment with a structural blue. The tenerals, freshly emerged adults, are often muted or pale in colour, gradually developing their adult colouration over a matter of days, and some species are pruinose, having a powdery looking appearance. This 'pruinescence' is due to a surface covering of a fine, waxy bloom.

Damselflies

Damselflies are much smaller and more delicate than dragonflies and are often found in large congregations in foliage such as grasses and brackens, roosting in the sun and taking off *en masse* as you walk past them, making them look like hundreds of tiny fairies fluttering around.

For a few weeks every spring and summer, walking around the Somerset Levels will be rewarded with some incredible views and, if you set your alarm early and are out around sunrise, you can often see them covered in dew, a wonderful time to photograph them. With care and patience you can achieve some beautiful images head-on with these characterful little animals. The more time you spend observing them the more photo opportunities you will recognise.

I love being on the reserve before sunrise and in the summer it is always light enough to be able to find damselflies before the sun rises allowing me to get into position and ready. Mornings on the Somerset Levels are often met with blankets of dew of varying thickness and I've only even been out once to find no dew at that time in the morning. Dew covers everything including the little damselflies, of which there are many to choose from. I am always looking for different perspectives and this individual was perfectly placed to allow me to capture a few different images; both "A Light In The Dark" and "Sunrise" are exactly the same damselfly taken 9 minutes apart either side of sunrise, one capturing the damselfly and grass covered in dew and the other capturing the damselfly silhouetted against the rising sun.

A Light In The Dark

Blue tailed damselfly (*Ischnura elegans*)
Canon 5D Mark III with Sigma 180mm f/2.8 macro lens, Gitzo tripod and head
Aperture f/2.8 | ISO 400 | Shutter speed 1/50sec

Sunrise

Blue tailed damselfly (*Ischnura elegans*)
Canon 5D Mark III with Sigma 180mm f/2.8 macro lens, Gitzo tripod and head.
Aperture f/2.8 | ISO 400 | Shutter speed 1/8000sec

Does My Nose Look Big In This

Following a night of rain and dew, the grass and its inhabitants were very wet. The one thing rain gives you that you don't get so much with dew is large water droplets. I found this common blue damselfly with a very large water droplet—in relation to the damselfly anyway—right on the end of its head, so when seen front-on it looked like it had a big nose. I used an aperture of f/10 to bring the water drop and as much of the eyes into focus as possible whilst trying to keep the background out of focus. Photographing damselflies this early in the morning has its challenges as they are low down in the grasses often in sheltered areas so a very carefully placed tripod is essential.

Common Blue Damselfly (*Enallagma cyathigerum*)
Canon 5D Mark III with Sigma 180mm f/2.8 macro lens, Gitzo tripod and head.
Aperture f/10 | ISO 500 | Shutter speed 1/15sec

Peek-a-Boo

For me, damselflies are some of the most charismatic of the invertebrates—you only have to spend a few hours with them to fall in love with their adorable little faces—and you can actually play peek-a-boo with them. On this reserve there are a lot of tall ferns upon which the damselflies congregate. They will peek through the fronds at you, the ferns making for wonderful green backgrounds that contrast beautifully with the blues of the damselflies. I sat for some time with this one as it peeked out from the back of the fern to look at me. The important thing is to be as still as possible and, when you do move, do so slowly.

Common Blue Damselfly (*Enallagma cyathigerum*)
Canon 5D Mark III with Sigma 180mm f/2.8 macro lens, Gitzo tripod and head.
Aperture f/4.5 | ISO 500 | Shutter speed 1/160sec

King Of The Swingers

Before they can take to the wing, damselflies must be dry and warmed up. I found this red-eyed damselfly hanging from the grass when it was still covered in dew, so I set up my tripod and waited for it to dry out. There was a light breeze, which made things a little tricky as damselflies are so light and easily blown around. I manually focused for this shot to allow me to achieve focus on the eyes, then it was a case of shooting as it passed by the front of the lens. It really did look as if the damselfly was swinging on the grass!

Red-Eyed Damselfly (*Erythromma najas*)
Canon 5D Mark III with Sigma 180mm f/2.8 macro lens, Gitzo tripod and head.
Aperture f/9 | ISO 500 | Shutter speed 1/160sec

Just Chilling

Damselflies are less active than dragonflies and, even when warmed up, often rest for a while on grasses or, in the case of this individual, on a small rock in the middle of the path. Naturally I laid down on the path to be at eye level, which truth be told is really not that comfy when it's gravel and small rocks, but it was well worth it to be able to capture this damselfly looking very relaxed.

Azure Damselfly (*Coenagrion puella*)
Canon 5D Mark III with Sigma 180mm f/2.8 macro lens
Aperture f/9 | ISO 640 | Shutter speed 1/100sec

Carefully Balanced

As the day warms up, the damselflies make their way up the grass stems towards the sunlight to warm up in turn. This can be a great opportunity to capture them head on with their wings out behind them, but it is tricky and requires patience; I would definitely recommend using a tripod as bending over holding a camera and lens is not great for the back and you'll probably find yourself swaying! To achieve this shot I used live view, zoomed in and manually focused to make sure the eyes and face were in focus, settling for an aperture that would bring enough detail into the shape of the wings and body whilst keeping the background blurred.

Common Blue Damselfly (*Enallagma cyathigerum*)
Canon 5D Mark III with Sigma 180mm f/2.8 macro lens, Gitzo tripod and head.
Aperture f/5.6 | ISO 500 | Shutter speed 1/60sec

Lunchtime

Damselflies are voracious predators and are important hunters of other flying invertebrates. They help to keep in check the numbers of potential pest species as well as biting flies, midges and mosquitoes. If you pick a spot, watch and wait, you will hopefully be rewarded with one having lunch right in front of you.

Common Blue Damselfly (*Enallagma cyathigerum*)
Canon 5D Mark III with Sigma 180mm f/2.8 macro lens, Gitzo tripod and head.
Aperture f/7.1 | ISO 500 | Shutter speed 1/160sec

Dragonflies

Dragonflies are larger than damselflies, voracious predators and expert fliers that have evolved some incredible adaptations.

Dragonfly wings have a 'wing mark' (pterostigma) on the leading edge of each wing which helps stabilise the wing and prevent vibrations during flight by acting as a weight. In addition to this they also possess a rib-like 'costa' along the leading edge, making it the strongest part of the wing and aiding the dragonfly in cutting through the air. These adaptations make dragonflies expert fliers, travelling up to 36 km/h, moving up and down, changing direction quickly and even hovering, all of which are vital to their survival as they hunt by catching prey in flight using their legs.

The eyes of dragonflies can detect colour, ultraviolet light, movement and the plane of polarisation. They have compound eyes with thousands of lens-covered units giving them wrap around vision: they have almost 360-degree vision with a blind spot only directly behind the eyes.

Dragonflies can be tricky to photograph and especially to find new angles or compositions, but if you head out early on chilly spring/summer mornings you can find them roosting in the long grass or dense foliage providing some different points of view. When I do find dragonflies in the long grass, I am very careful going about photographing them. I will never move them or garden around them, instead I will shoot through the foliage and where I may have flattened some grass I will also pull it back up again.

Group Roost

Occasionally, four-spotted chasers will congregate in large groups to roost but it is unclear exactly as to why they do this. I'm lucky to have one such roost relatively close by. For a few weeks each year they roost in their hundreds if not thousands, sometimes in one particular area, dispersing once warmed up in the morning. For someone that gets excited at finding a couple of dragonflies close together, seeing hundreds roosting at one site is just mind blowing. These roosts are a mix of females and males, which makes it even more surprising as males are extremely territorial, usually chasing away anything that comes into their territory with the exception of females. Yet here in these roosts they seem to tolerate one another. If you are lucky to see one of these mass roosts it can be overwhelming when it comes to photographing them, what with the confusion of bodies, legs and wings. To capture this scene I decided on a black and white image that would illustrate the jumble of dragonflies (actually I took several hundred images in the end but I needed to pick one). As soon as the sun rises it lights up this part of the reserve first, which may be one reason they roost in this spot; they can be warmed and on the wing before other parts of the reserve are even in sunlight.

Four-Spotted Chaser (*Libellula quadrimaculata*)
Canon 5D Mark III with Sigma 180mm f/2.8 macro lens
Aperture f/2.8 | ISO 640 | Shutter speed 1/400sec

Pink Glow

Away from the group roost there were a fair few individuals roosting separately in amongst the tall grasses. On this particular day, just before the sun rose, there was a soft, pink glow that bathed the area and some of the dragonflies in light. The light was just stunning and so soft, adding a little bit of magic to the morning. Shooting in quite a congested area, I used a wide aperture to blur out some of the details in the background to give a more dreamy effect.

Four-Spotted Chaser (*Libellula quadrimaculata*)
Canon 5D Mark III with Sigma 180mm f/2.8 macro lens
Aperture f/2.8 | ISO 800 | Shutter speed 1/50sec

All A Flutter

As the sun rises and the day starts to warm up, the dragonflies slowly crawl their way up the stems and out of the cover of the vegetation. I watched this individual for half an hour as it made its way to the top of a stem, by which time much of the dew had already disappeared from its body and wings. As it reached the top it started to beat its wings to remove the remaining dew in readiness for flight. I was amazed at just how still the body stays as it beats it wings (at about 30 beats per second); I wanted to partly freeze this moment but at the same time having a bit of movement too. With the dragonfly backlit, I was able to isolate it against a dark background for greater impact.

Four-Spotted Chaser (*Libellula quadrimaculata*)
Canon 5D Mark III with Sigma 180mm f/2.8 macro lens, Gitzo tripod and head.
Aperture f/9 | ISO 1250 | Shutter speed 1/2000sec

Veins

The wings of the dragonfly are a thing of beauty and being able to silhouette a dragonfly against the sky to show those details is something that I have been looking to photograph for a while. However, finding a suitable dragonfly in a suitable position was tricky. I eventually found one and it was on a slightly overcast day giving a white background to allow me to silhouette the dragonfly and enabling me to use a small aperture to bring everything into focus. I had the time to compose the image in a few different ways but sometimes I like to use negative space in my images rather than fill the frame.

Four-Spotted Chaser (*Libellula quadrimaculata*)
Canon 5D Mark III with Sigma 180mm f/2.8 macro lens, Gitzo tripod and head.
Aperture f/16 | ISO 400 | Shutter speed 1/320sec

Silver Wings

The sunrise to dragonflies is the start of their day; the warmth dries them out and heats their bodies, enabling them to take to the wing in search of food and a mate. It is this moment at the beginning of the day as well as the important role the sun plays in the life of the dragonfly that I was looking to capture. The sun rises from behind a bank of trees which, being in shadow, naturally gives a dark background, allowing for a high contrast image. I sat for some time waiting for this fleeting moment where the dragonfly was backlit by the rising sun, giving a silver appearance to the wings as the remaining dew dried. I used a small aperture to bring as much detail into focus as I could. I went for black and white for this image for a greater impact and to really draw the eye to the details of the dragonfly.

Four-Spotted Chaser (*Libellula quadrimaculata*)
Canon 5D Mark III with Sigma 180mm f/2.8 macro lens, Gitzo tripod and head.
Aperture f/18 | ISO 640 | Shutter speed 1/8000sec

Edges

Hiding deep in amongst the long grasses of the Somerset Levels are dragonflies, and the early mornings of May find these insects covered in hundreds if not thousands of tiny dew drops. I have spent many early mornings with these dragonflies getting very wet at times and wanted to illustrate just how well they disappear into the long grasses by just having the very edge of the wings in focus but with enough depth to the image to show the outline of the body behind. This image was manually focused to achieve sharpness just to the wing edges.

Four-Spotted Chaser (*Libellula quadrimaculata*)
Canon 5D Mark III with Sigma 180mm f/2.8 macro lens, Gitzo tripod and head.
Aperture f/4 | ISO 320 | Shutter speed 1/200sec

Hiding In The Grass

Sometimes, it would seem the dragonflies come to you when you least expect it. Whilst photographing another invertebrate, this black tailed skimmer flew in and landed on the grass in front of where I was lying. I used the grass in front of my lens to create the blur in the foreground and a wide aperture to bring some detail into the rest of the grass whilst focusing on the dragonfly. I actually like to obscure parts of my subject occasionally as it shows how well they can blend in sometimes.

Black-Tailed Skimmer (*Orthetrum cancellatum*)
Canon 5D Mark III with Sigma 180mm f/2.8 macro lens, Gitzo tripod and head.
Aperture f/2.8 | ISO 250 | Shutter speed 1/3200sec

Sparkle

Some mornings when you head out on to the reserve it can be tricky to find the dragonflies; this female was the only dragonfly I found one morning, the only thing giving her away being the sparkle of the light hitting all the tiny dew drops on her wings. Dragonflies are one of our most photographed invertebrates, right up there with butterflies, so trying to find new angles and perspectives can be hard. As it was the sparkle of the wings that first caught my eye with this female, it was that which I used as my inspiration for this image, focusing not on the eye or head of the dragonfly but on her wings, using a wide aperture to blur out her body and create the textures in the background.

Black Tailed Skimmer (*Orthetrum cancellatum*)
Canon 5D Mark III with Sigma 180mm f/2.8 macro lens, Gitzo tripod and head.
Aperture f/4 | ISO 250 | Shutter speed 1/1000sec

In The Slag Piles

The common darter is one of the later species, emerging in mid- to late summer, with individuals often still seen into November in some years. These are one of the few dragonflies that make the slag piles on the Mendip Hills their territory, with both males and females being seen resting and feeding in amongst the foliage that grows there. This is not the most ideal of places to try and photograph them as I can honestly say it isn't very comfy lying on the rocks and I do recommend elbow and knee pads. I've spent a couple of years photographing this population of common darters and have found they can be rather fearless, often landing on you. They are surprisingly easy to observe and photograph if you lie on the ground at their eye level. I love this habitat to photograph them in as there are so many different colours from the unique, metal tolerant plants. These provide a perfect backdrop, blending so wonderfully with the dragonflies and especially with their eyes.

Common Darter (*Sympetrum striolatum*)
Canon 5D Mark III with Canon 100mm f/2.8 macro lens, Gitzo tripod and head.
Aperture f/2.8 | ISO 200 | Shutter speed 1/60sec

Other Invertebrates

Covered in Pollen

Brassy mining bees, as with all bees, are important pollinators of wildflowers and economically important food plants. These are small bees, as you can see from this photograph of one on speedwell covered in pollen.

Despite there being a fair few of these bees around, the conditions were less than ideal for photographing them as it was so windy. But persistence and a slight drop in wind paid off eventually and by using a wide aperture and focusing on the eye of the bee I could blur out the background. It is always good to take a step back a little sometimes and actually show some of the habitat and plants, giving your subject a little more space rather than getting right in close.

Brassy mining bee (*Lasioglossum morio*)
Canon 5D Mark III with Canon 100mm f/2.8 macro lens
Aperture f/2.8 | ISO 200 | Shutter speed 1/400sec

Sunrise

Sunrise in the grasslands is an important time for so many invertebrates, especially following a chilly night, as it allows them to dry out and warm up ready for the day ahead. On my numerous trips to the chalk grasslands, I have only found the speckled bush cricket a couple of times on the top of flowers or seed heads as they are normally further down in the vegetation. Finding this one covered in dew drops, I was able to carefully set everything up in time to photograph it against the rising sun coming through the trees; I used a small LED light to add additional light to just the cricket and flower heads. Speckled bush crickets blend in very well to the surrounding vegetation thanks to their colouration and markings. Unlike some other species of cricket, when the male calls, the female is able to respond with a weak call of her own, but these calls are almost inaudible to humans and are best heard with the aid of a bat detector.

Speckled bush-cricket (Leptophyes punctatissima)
Canon 5D Mark III with Canon 100mm f/2.8 macro lens, Gitzo tripod and head, Manfrotto Lumimuse 6 with diffusers
Aperture f/5.6 | ISO 400 | Shutter speed 1/160sec

In The Daisies

This tiny, dark bush cricket nymph was found in my garden amongst the common daisies, giving you an idea of just how teeny tiny it is. It was tricky to get a shot of it as every time I picked up the camera it would move to the underneath of the flower. However, after much playing of peek-a-boo with it, I was able to grab a shot as it peeked its head up through the petals. I used the surrounding daisies to frame the cricket and to show it in its habitat rather than simply taking a close-up shot.

Adult dark bush crickets have two different calls, one to attract mates and an intimidation call to warn off rival males; should males end up fighting they 'fence' with their antennae

Dark Bush Cricket (*Pholidoptera griseoaptera*)
Canon 5D Mark III with Sigma 180mm f/2.8 macro lens
Aperture f/4.5 | ISO 400 | Shutter speed 1/125sec

Is it a grasshopper or a cricket?

The easiest way to tell the difference is by looking at the antennae; grasshoppers have shorter, thicker antennae whereas those of crickets are thinner and much longer. The way they produce the chirping sound (stridulation) differs also; grasshoppers rub their hind legs against their wings whereas crickets rub their wings together.

I've had many people ask me how to photograph both grasshoppers and crickets as they struggle and the simple answer is practice and patience. You should also photograph them from their eye level; this will give you a connection with them and make them a lot less jumpy.

I'm So Cute

There is something delightfully appealing about both grasshopper and cricket nymphs that is lacking in the adults. They are a challenge to photograph mainly because of their size; this nymph is on a nettle leaf and you can see the tiny hairs of the leaf, giving you an idea of its size. I spent over an hour with this little nymph photographing it from various different angles, but this is by far my favourite image. The combination of the nymph looking straight at the camera and the colours and lines of the leaves bring it all together for me and make that little nymph look just too cute.

Meadow Grasshopper (*Chorthippus parallelus*)
Canon 7D with Canon 100mm f/2.8 macro lens
Aperture f/5 | ISO 400 | Shutter speed 1/250sec

Hmm Let me Think

Grasshoppers of all stages have so much character and although they lose some of that cuteness as they mature, they more than make up for it in their other expressions. When I come across a grasshopper I will spend a fair bit of time with it, watching and occasionally taking some shots, they will often use their fronts legs to wipe their eyes and these moments are wonderful, producing some great comical and caption worthy images like this one.

To me this one looks like its scratching its head whilst having a think. Although there are some that think we shouldn't anthropomorphise animals, it is a great way to encourage people to see them differently and to engage more with these less-loved species, not to mention a wonderful way to spark the interest of children.

Common Field Grasshopper (*Chorthippus brunneus*)
Canon 5D Mark III with Canon 100mm f/2.8 macro lens
Aperture f/6.3 | ISO 400 | Shutter speed 1/125sec

Can You See Me?

The rufous grasshopper is a nationally scarce species and I'm very lucky to have a small population of them close to home living on a chalk grassland. At first glance they are similar in appearance to a couple of other species, but if you look closely at the antennae you will notice white tips to them, which gives away their identity. In late summer you may even be lucky enough to witness their courtship display, wherein the males waggle their antennae at the females, however the females are very picky resulting in many failed display attempts by the males.

One thing I do love about these grasshoppers is that they will sit and watch you watch them if you are at eye level or below. During late summer and early autumn the colours of the rufous grasshopper blend almost perfectly with those of the dry grasslands, especially in the low morning sun. I sat for some time with this individual waiting for it to appear from behind the seed head and it was well worth waiting for. As with much wildlife photography, waiting can be an integral part of getting the shot.

Rufous Grasshopper (*Gomphocerippus rufus*)
Canon 7D with Canon 100mm f/2.8 macro lens, Gitzo tripod and head
Aperture f/5.6 | ISO 400 | Shutter speed 1/125sec

Climbing The Moss Mountain

Oil beetles are fascinating nest parasites of solitary mining bees. Their tiny larvae attach to suitable bees as they visit flowers and are transported back to the nest where they feed on the pollen stores.

I found this individual slowly making its way up the side of a moss covered rock, occasionally stopping and moving its head around before continuing the climb. These small pauses allowed me to capture the incredible colour and details of the beetle in the sunlight

Violet Oil Beetle (*Meloe violaceus*)
Canon 7D with Canon 100mm f/2.8 macro lens
Aperture f/10 | ISO 400 | Shutter speed 1/80sec

Pretty In Pink

Have you ever seen a pink grasshopper? If you have, did you wonder why it was pink?

A couple of years ago I came across a couple of pink grasshoppers locally, but the first time I had actually seen such things was in the Carpathian Mountains of Romania, which prompted me to investigate further. The pink colouration is an unusual and little-understood genetic mutation called erythrism. It is caused by a recessive gene similar to that which affects albino animals. This mutation results in one of two things happening, or even a combination of the two; a reduction or even absence of the normal pigment and/or the excessive production of other pigments—in this case red—which results in pink morphs. Although it was first discovered in 1887 in a katydid species, it is extremely rare to see these pink morphs as they are more easily picked off by predators. As you can see, this pink grasshopper is really conspicuous against the fresh green growth of the gorse.

Meadow Grasshopper (*Chorthippus parallelus*)
Canon 7D with Canon 100mm f/2.8 macro lens
Aperture f/5.6 | ISO 400 | Shutter speed 1/640sec

The Weevil and The Fern

Green nettle weevils can be seen throughout the summer on various different types of plant, but particularly nettles, from which it gets its name. They have a brilliant metallic green colour which comes from the densely packed scales that cover its black body; these scales rub off with age to reveal the black underneath. I came across this weevil on the bracken and watched as it walked up and down the fronds and then stopped, carefully balanced on the frond. With another frond in the background, the image is completed. The Weevil and The Fern sounds to me rather like a wonderful children's story.

Green Nettle Weevil (*Phyllobius pomaceus*)
Canon 30D with Canon 100mm f/2.8 macro lens
Aperture f/4.5 | ISO 400 | Shutter speed 1/320sec

Mossy Adventure

The bloody-nosed beetle is flightless and one of the first beetles I see out and about in springtime as they wander around in search of a mate. They get their common name from the bright red, foul-tasting liquid they exude from their mouths when threatened. The males have much larger tarsal pads which they use to grip the female's carapace during mating and you can often see pairs of the them walking around in the springtime.

This is a male (notice the orange tarsal pads) found amongst moss-covered rocks in early springtime. I positioned myself at eye level with him so I could capture him coming through the moss towards me

Bloody Nosed Beetle (*Timarcha tenebricosa*)
Canon 5D Mark III with Canon 100mm f/2.8 macro lens
Aperture f/7.1 | ISO 320 | Shutter speed 1/160sec

Look At My Antennae

There really are some weird and wonderful little critters hiding in the long grass if you go looking for them. I came across this non-biting midge on a dew-covered blade of grass whilst on the search for spiders. I was captivated not only by the positioning and delicate way it was attached to the blade of grass amongst the dew but also by those very fluffy antennae. I experimented with the aperture to capture the details in the midge and surrounding dew drops whilst keeping the background blurred.

Non-Biting Midge (*Chironomidae*)
Canon 5D Mark III with Sigma 180mm f/2.8 macro lens
Aperture f/5 | ISO 500 | Shutter speed 1/320sec

Curious

Leaf hoppers are adorably cute little invertebrates that suck the sap out of plants, but they can be notoriously hard to photograph requiring a lot of patience to both find them and then to capture an image of one. The green leaf hopper is a large and common species of leaf hopper inhabiting marshy areas. They are often found low down in the vegetation.

I found this one by accident and settled to down to see what it did; although it moved around a fair bit, it stayed in the immediate area which allowed me to carefully move myself into a position to photograph it. I found that by photographing it from slightly below it seemed a little less jumpy and would move around the grass stem, pausing at various different angles.

Being amongst the grasses it was quite a congested area, but by using an aperture of f/5 I was able to blur out the surrounding vegetation, with the leaf hopper peering out of the image

Green Leaf Hopper (*Cicadella viridis*)
Canon 7D with Canon 100mm f/2.8 macro lens
Aperture f/5 | ISO 400 | Shutter speed 1/250sec

Mating Bubbles

Yellow dung flies are a common sight in the countryside and can be found in a variety of habitats. This pair was actually on a tree in my parents' garden and after watching for a short while I noticed that the pair were blowing bubbles as they mated. This bubbling is actually a regurgitation of liquid from the crop, resulting in the formation of a droplet on the proboscis which is then sucked back in. The exact reason for this behaviour remains unclear.

For whatever reason they carry out this bubbling behaviour, it did make for a fascinating and different image that only works as a black and white silhouette as it brings out all the details in both the flies and the bubbles. Both flies are bubbling; the male's bubble is obvious, but look closely and you will see the tiny bubble starting to form on the female too.

Yellow Dung Fly (*Scathophaga stercoraria*)
Canon 7D with Canon 100mm f/2.8 macro lens
Aperture f/9 | ISO 500 | Shutter speed 1/200sec

Late summer/early autumn brings with it craneflies—and lots of them in some areas—particularly in the meadows, but they seem to get a hard time of it, being often seen as harmful when they stray into our houses.

However they don't bite and, in fact, most don't feed at all in the adult stage. As flying adults they are harmless, but during the larval stage large populations can be damaging to lawns. But there is something endearing about these gangly flies, especially when you see them close up with their big eyes (which are emerald green in some species) and halteres (modified hind wings that act as highly sophisticated balance organs that oscillate during flight).

Cranefly Sparkle

An early morning in late September on the Somerset Levels reveals a thick blanket of dew, amongst which are craneflies, slowly making their way upwards out of the long grass to dry out in the sun. They can be easily missed as they blend in so well with the long grass but I found this one in a lovely position at the edge of a grassy patch. This allowed me to capture a background bokeh and at the same time creating a sparkly effect with the sun lighting up the dew droplets on the cranefly and grass.

Cranefly (*Tipula* spp)
Canon 5D Mark III with Canon 100mm f/2.8 macro lens
Aperture f/9 | ISO 200 | Shutter speed 1/100sec

Harvestman are arachnids but not spiders, belonging to an order of their own (Opiliones); you can see some similarities with spiders, but they lack both venom and silk glands and the body is just one part versus two in spiders.

There is no denying that they are very odd looking creatures, but they have been around for 400 million years. Many species have their eyes on the top of their body on a bump called an ocularium. If you watch a harvestman for any length of time you will notice that the second pair of legs is longer than the others and are constantly moving around; these contain sensory organs that allow them to feel their surroundings

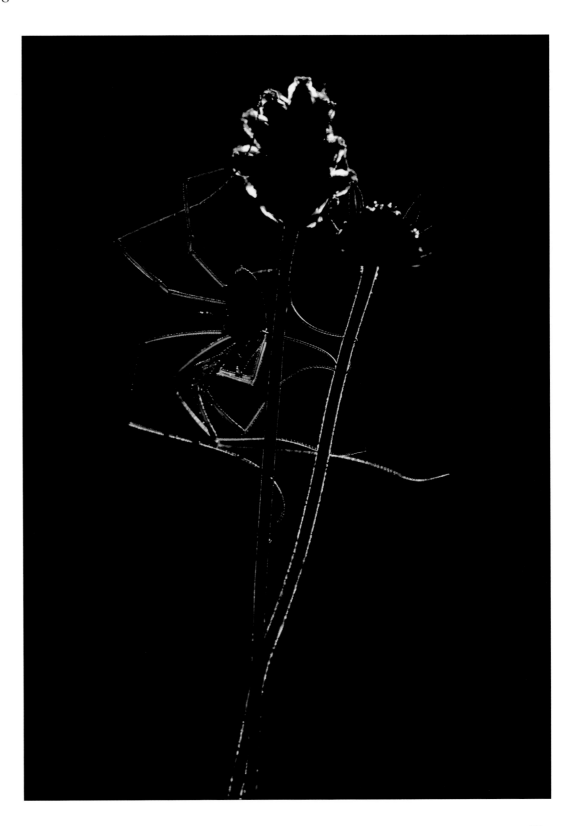

Legs Of Light

I love being out in the countryside first thing in the morning; it's so peaceful and you get to witness some incredible sunrises. It is also a great time to photograph invertebrates and that first light in August is just beautiful. It's not often you find a harvestman high up in the long grasses but this one was, and as the rising sun shone through the trees it highlighted the tiny dew drops that had formed overnight and lit up the legs of the harvestman

Harvestman (*Opiliones* spp)
Canon 5D with Sigma 180mm f/2.8 macro lens
Aperture f/9 | ISO 400 | Shutter speed 1/500sec

Lurking

The common crab spider gets its name from the crab-like movements it makes and if you sit and watch one for a while you can observe these movements quite easily. Crab spiders are ambush predators that sit and wait for their prey to come to them. I found this one lurking amongst the long grasses surrounded by damselflies, waiting with its legs ready and open for an unsuspecting invertebrate to come within reach. Interestingly, when these crab spiders mate, the male holds onto one of the female's legs until she stops struggling then, using silk to tie her down, he crawls underneath to mate with her.

Crab Spider (*Xysticus cristatus*)
Canon 5D Mark III with Sigma 180mm f/2.8 macro lens
Aperture f/4 | ISO 400 | Shutter speed 1/640sec

What Big Eyes You Have

The jumping spider must win the award for most adorably cute spider with its large, dark eyes. Jumping spiders actively hunt their prey and have some of the best vision in the spider world; when they find a potential meal they jump by increasing the blood flow to their legs, causing them to extend and pushing them into the air. I found this tiny little spider whilst doing a butterfly survey and was completely distracted watching it move around the seed head. I waited until it popped up facing me to take the photograph.

Jumping Spider (*Sitticus pubescens*)
Canon 5D Mark III with Canon 100mm f/2.8 macro lens
Aperture f/2.8 | ISO 400 | Shutter speed 1/320sec

It's a Big Scary World Out There... for a Little Spider

Spider's silk is nature's strongest material but it is not just used for weaving webs as not all spiders actually weave them; it is used to produce egg sacs, to wrap prey, form draglines, for parachuting or ballooning, and to form shelters or fulfil certain roles in mating. I found this wolf spider in my parent's garden and sat and watched it for a while as it came and went, stopping occasionally. It paused just long enough in a patch of light, seemingly looking up at the leaf or what was on the leaf, to allow me to grab this shot from side on.

Wolf Spider (*Pardosa* spp)
Canon 30D with Canon 100mm f/2.8 macro lens
Aperture f/7.1 | ISO 320 | Shutter speed 1/60sec

Web Of Beauty

Spiders produce silk from glands, of which there are seven different types, but not all spiders have all seven; males have at least three, while females have at least four (the fourth is for egg sacs). The glands are located on the underside of the abdomen and contain a watery fluid that passes through the spinnerets, each of which can move independently of each other. The silk itself is made up of protein and is emitted as a liquid that hardens as a result of the drawing-out process which alters the molecular structure. Each thread is composed of several fibres drawn out from separate spigots (openings of the silk glands in the spinnerets) forming a cable-like thread. Spiders eat their own webs to recycle the proteins in readiness for the weaving of a new web, which they do every day.

This female moved her web ever so slightly each day and on the day I took this image I was able to achieve an angle that allowed me to shoot through her dew-covered web, manually focusing on her and using the lines of silk to draw the eye towards her in the centre of the web.

Garden Cross Spider (*Araneus diadematus*)
Canon 5D Mark III with Canon 100mm f/2.8 macro lens, Gitzo tripod and head
Aperture f/6.3 | ISO 400 | Shutter speed 1/50sec

Zombie Snail

Zombie snails are something that until recently I had only seen on TV, but as luck would have it I actually came across one for real in 2016. A zombie snail is actually an Amber snail (*Succinea putris*) parasitized by *Leucochloridium* spp. The snail eats the eggs of the flatworm and the larvae develop filling the eye stalks making them look like wriggling caterpillars, often the snails will be much more out in the open than uninfected ones, attracting bird which the parasite needs for the next stage of its life cycle.

Amber snail (*Succinea putris*) parasitised by a *Leucochloridium* sp.
Canon 5D with Sigma 180mm f/2.8 macro lens
Aperture f/4.5 | ISO 500 | Shutter speed 1/250sec

The worm in its larval, miracidia stage, travels into the digestive system of a snail to develop into the next stage, sporocyst. The sporocyst grows into long tubes to form swollen "broodsacs" filled with tens to hundreds of cercariae. These broodsacs invade the snail's tentacles causing a brilliant transformation of the tentacles into a swollen, pulsating, colourful display that mimics the appearance of a caterpillar or grub. Infected snails are often called zombie snails.

Amber snail (*Succinea putris*) parasitised by a *Leucochloridium* sp.
Canon 5D with Sigma 180mm f/2.8 macro lens
Aperture f/3.5 | ISO 320 | Shutter speed 1/250sec

Amphibians

Amphibians are wonderfully characterful animals that we mainly encounter as they emerge from hibernation in early spring, gathering at ponds to breed. We later see their young in the summer as they leave the ponds following metamorphosis. 'Amphibian' comes from the Greek meaning "both kinds of life", since most species need water to reproduce and require moisture to survive but are capable of living on land. They are an important evolutionary link between water-dwelling fish and land-dwelling reptiles and mammals.

You will notice that the majority of my amphibian images are taken at eye level, where possible, which allows me to have a better connections with my subjects that really bring out their characters. It also means getting very wet, muddy, stung and bitten, but it's well worth it to spend time with these wonderful little animals

Common Frogs (*Rana temporaria*)

Frogs generally return to the ponds they were born in and females may lay up to 4,000 eggs in clumps of spawn. It takes approximately 12 weeks for metamorphosis of tadpoles into frogs, at which point the little froglets leave the ponds to start their frog lives. Only about 5 out of 2,000 tadpoles manage to metamorphose; those that survive will reach sexual maturity at around 3 years.

Frogs are often found in damper areas of their habitat (outside of the breeding season) as they don't drink, but actually absorb water through their skin. It is through their skin that half of their breathing also takes place, so it's important to keep it moist.

Emerging From The Pond

Young common frog carefully making its way out of the pond. Laying on the ground to be at eye level with the frog I used a wide aperture to blur everything except the eyes as it looked directly towards me with the light reflecting off the water and wet mud creating a wonderful bokeh for the frog to emerge from.

Common frog (*Rana temporaria*)
Canon 5D Mark III with Sigma 180mm f/2.8 macro lens
Aperture f/2.8 | ISO 400 | Shutter speed 1/1600 sec

Common frogs are a welcome visitor to gardens for many due to their predation of snails, slugs and other invertebrates. Frogs have a long sticky tongue which they use to catch unsuspecting invertebrates, while their saliva is a non-Newtonian fluid, behaving as both a liquid and a solid. As the tongue makes contact with its prey, the saliva is more liquid allowing it to engulf the prey, but as the tongue retracts, the saliva momentarily thickens, drawing the prey with it and making it harder for the prey to escape.

Exploring

This is a young and rather pale common frog I found in our garden as I was clearing an area to create a mini wildflower meadow and wildlife pond. I sat and watched for a while as it moved around in amongst the plants and as it faced away from me I captured this shot from behind as it lifted its front leg towards a twig, I used a wide aperture to bring the focus to the eye of the frog.

Common frog (*Rana temporaria*)
Canon 5D Mark III with Sigma 180mm f/2.8 macro lens
Aperture f/2.8 | ISO 400 | Shutter speed 1/2500 sec

Fancy Seeing You Here

On hot days in the summer you can often find common frogs near to the ponds as they use the water to cool off. It was on such a day that I came across this little frog making its way to the pond across a stony path. So naturally I laid down on the path and watched as it made its way, photographing it as it went. At one point it started heading straight for me, advancing through the tiny blades of grass that were growing up through the path.

Common frog (*Rana temporaria*)
Canon 5D Mark III with Sigma 180mm f/2.8 macro lens
Aperture f/4.5 | ISO 250 | Shutter speed 1/640 sec

Hiding In The Primroses

Garden ponds occasionally need some maintenance carried out and with the help of my brother we cleared out some areas of our parents pond, during which we came across a few frogs and noticed some wounds on their legs, we carefully examined and photographed these before releasing them. We left this one to make its way back to the pond, as it did so it popped its head up in amongst the primroses that grow around the pond.

Common frog (*Rana temporaria*)
Canon 5D Mark III with Canon 100mm f/2.8 macro lens
Aperture f/2.8 | ISO 400 | Shutter speed 1/400 sec

New Home

When we moved into our new house I had a plan of putting in a small wildlife pond, something that took me over a year to complete, but within days of finishing the pond this little frog moved in. I had seen this little frog a few times in the garden poking out from underneath the decking and it shows that you don't need a big pond just something small that they can use to cool off on hot days. I'm hoping that maybe next year the frogs will spawn in the pond.

Common frog (*Rana temporaria*)
Canon 5D Mark III with Sigma 180mm f/2.8 macro lens
Aperture f/4.5 | ISO 200 | Shutter speed 1/160 sec

Spawn
Frogs have to start somewhere, and that is here as spawn. Frogs will return in the early spring to the ponds in which they were born a few years before to breed and continue the cycle. Frog spawn can be tricky to photograph; this year the frogs returned after four years away to breed in the garden pond, which gave me the chance to try different angles and lighting. Frog spawn is best photographed soon after it has been laid and on slightly overcast days as bright sunlight will reflect off both the water and frog spawn. I opted for a high contrast black and white image to offer something different and draw the eye to the structure of the egg and its unexpected beauty.

Common frog (*Rana temporaria*)
Canon 5D Mark III with Sigma 180mm f/2.8 macro lens
Aperture f/4.5 | ISO 640 | Shutter speed 1/200 sec

Perez's Frog (*Pelophylax perezi*)

The Perez's or Iberian water frog is not a species native to the UK but it is now a naturalised species on the Somerset Levels providing an additional food source for the many migratory and resident birds. They are easily distinguished from our common frogs as they are nearly always found in or on the edges of the ponds. They also vary in colour being much brighter and with a degree of bright green colour. That said they do vary greatly in colour from dark brown through to bright green but nearly always have a bright green stripe that runs from their head along the dorsal side.

Photographing Perez's frogs is challenging as they are far more jumpy than common frogs and as you walk along the paths you hear the tell tale 'plop' sound as they leap into the water.

Eyes

Once the frogs leap into the water they stay submerged for a few minutes before popping their eyes and nose through the surface. To make the eyes really stand out, I used an ISO of 50 and long exposure to smooth out the water. The image was taken in the late afternoon, so the frog is lit by the low autumn sun, bringing a sparkle to its eyes.

Perez's frog (*Pelophylax perezi*)
Canon 5D Mark III with Sigma 180mm f/2.8 macro lens
Aperture f/4.5 | ISO 50 | Shutter speed 1/80 sec

Over several months observing Perez's frogs at various times of the day and trying different field craft skills, I finally managed to find a way to creep in close to them allowing me to achieve some intimate images and photograph some very interesting behaviours.

Hmm Tasty

I laid watching this frog for some time as it seemed to have something in its mouth, but after much observing and research it turns out it was actually eating its own skin: dermatophagy. They do this by inflating themselves and then using their hind legs to push the skin forwards towards their front legs and then eventually into their mouths. It is thought that they do this to recycle the nutrients within the skin. It is an incredible behaviour to observe and this image shows the frog inflated with its hind legs raised, ready to scrape the skin forwards.

Perez's frog (*Pelophylax perezi*)
Canon 5D Mark III with Sigma 180mm f/2.8 macro lens
Aperture f/9 | ISO 250 | Shutter speed 1/60 sec

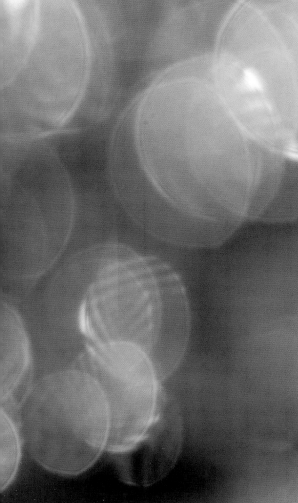

Frog's Eye

Frogs have incredible eyes if you can get close enough to see them, which I managed after months of perfecting my field craft skills, getting very muddy, wet, hot and covered in scratches, but it was well worth it. Creeping up on this individual very carefully I was able to capture the eye from behind as it sat looking out over the pond with the soft sunlight creating a lovely bokeh in the background that is complimented by the sun reflecting off the back of the moist skin of the frog. To achieve the sharpness in the eye I had to manually focus this.

Perez's frog (*Pelophylax perezi*)
Canon 5D Mark III with Sigma 180mm f/2.8 macro lens
Aperture f/2.8 | ISO 320 | Shutter speed 1/640 sec

Hiding

If you can't see any Perez's frogs on the banks of the ponds, chances are they are hiding in amongst the plants. They are surprisingly well camouflaged and you can see how well the mottled patterns come in to play. I've noticed that for a large proportion of the time when they are in amongst the plants they sit with just their eyes and nose above the water. One thing that really caught my eye with this frog was not so much the frog but the patterns and colours of the twigs and plants and the reflections in the water. I also noticed how well the colours complimented the little frog. Using a wide aperture I was able to limit the focus to a small area on the image allowing everything else to gently blur as you look outwards from the frog.

Perez's frog (*Pelophylax perezi*)
Canon 5D Mark III with Sigma 180mm f/2.8 macro lens
Aperture f/2.8 | ISO 400 | Shutter speed 1/5000 sec

Gazing

The Perez's frog are never too far from the water and can often be found in amongst the foliage on the banks of the ponds. After spending months with them, I had finally found a way to be able to photograph them at their level without disturbing them or them leaping into the water. Although most of the time they are motionless, every now and then they raise their heads looking upwards towards the sky. I've used a wide aperture to blur out the foreground and background drawing the attention to the frog's face as it gazes upwards leaving it plenty of space to look into, I've chosen monochrome for this image to really draw your attention to the frog.

Perez's frog (*Pelophylax perezi*)
Canon 5D Mark III with Sigma 180mm f/2.8 macro lens
Aperture f/3.5 | ISO 320 | Shutter speed 1/400 sec

Autumn Reflections

As you look into the ponds in the early evening, you can see the heads and eyes of the frogs just above the surface of the water. On a calm day they can be reflected almost perfectly. Towards the end of September, the autumn colours started to show on the bushes and trees at the back of the pond; the low evening sun enhanced these colours so that, when level with the water, they are reflected on the surface giving rise to a wonderful range of colours that compliment those of the frog's eyes.

Perez's frog (*Pelophylax perezi*)
Canon 5D Mark III with Sigma 180mm f/2.8 macro lens
Aperture f/3.5 | ISO 50 | Shutter speed 1/250 sec

Common Toad (*Bufo bufo*)

Common toads live in a wide variety of habitats and the colour of their skin closely matches that of their habitats, providing camouflage for this ambush predator. This also makes them tricky to see except during the breeding season. They are predominantly nocturnal except for during the breeding season when they are active day and night.

We first see toads as they emerge in early spring, sometimes as early as February depending on the weather, as they emerge from hibernation and start making the journey to their breeding ponds. The toad population I have spent the most time observing hibernates in woodlands and they have to cross an at times very busy road and head downhill to reach the breeding ponds. When they first start to emerge you find just a few individuals, but it doesn't take long before you have to be very careful walking the paths due to the sheer numbers of toads covering them.

The one thing that gives away a big toad breeding pond is the noise; males make quite an adorable squeaking sound when other males grasp them, a response that alerts the grasping toad to the fact that they are not female. The breeding season lasts just a few days, during which time some males will try to grasp pretty much anything, including my legs, arms, hands, tripod and lens, as well as each other.

Oh Hello

I think toads are such wonderful little creatures full of character. Having spent so much time with them, I want to try to capture the more amusing side to them—it wasn't as hard I had originally thought it might be. As I was setting up some soft lights for later in the evening, this male appeared from the grasses and sat on the path looking straight at me; laying half in the stream and half on the path, I composed the shot with the eyes just popping up into the frame.

Common Toad (*Bufo bufo*)
Canon 5D Mark III with Sigma 180mm f/2.8 macro lens with Manfrotto Lykos LED Panel
Aperture f/4 | ISO 200 | Shutter speed 1/200 sec

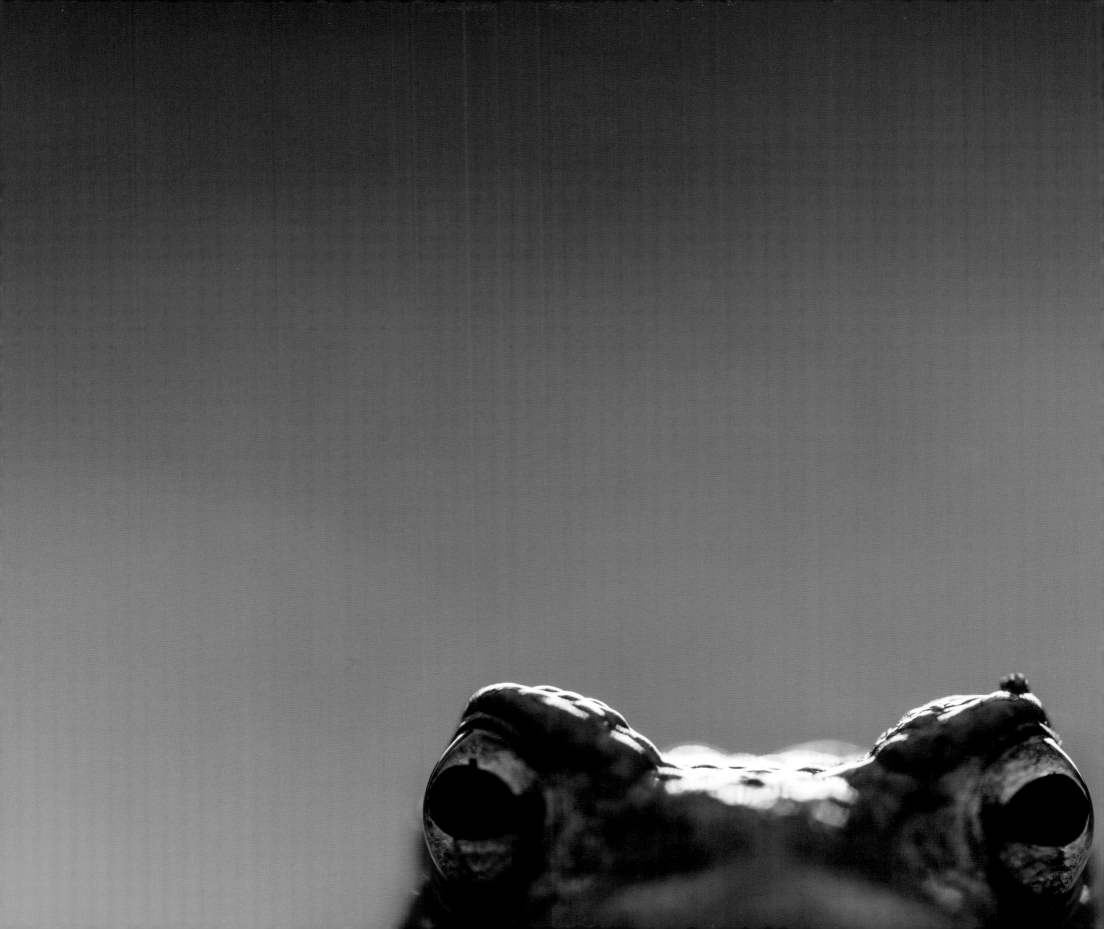

From the Muddy Puddle

As the weather warms and the toads start emerging from their hibernation sites, they have to make the journey to the breeding ponds. This normally involves travelling along the main path on the reserve, a path that is frequently dotted with large puddles at that time of year. This is one of the first toads I saw in 2017 and it was sitting in one of these puddles looking down the path; there was only one thing to do, lie flat on the path to photograph the toad. As I got myself into position, I noticed that if I angled myself just right I could capture the toad's reflection in the puddle and make it look almost as if it was emerging from the puddle itself. This toad sat in the same position from some time, which allowed me to experiment with the aperture to get just enough detail in the image.

Common Toad (*Bufo bufo*)
Canon 5D Mark III with Sigma 180mm f/2.8 macro lens
Aperture f/3.5 | ISO 500 | Shutter speed 1/250 sec

Mating Ball

Mating season is a couple of weeks of frantic activity at the breeding ponds, some years more than others, as hundreds of toads gather to breed. In 2016 breeding seemed particularly frantic compared to 2015 and 2017, with several mating balls forming in the main pond. I watched this particular ball for some time watching males come and go, fighting over prime positions and trying to knock each other off. Unfortunately they seemed not to notice that this female was already dead, most likely drowned by the sheer number of males attached to her; at one point there was at least twelve. Although I took numerous images of this scene, this image remains my favourite with the focus on the one large male and his eye with the front legs of the bloated female fading away into the image.

Common Toad (*Bufo bufo*)
Canon 5D Mark III with Canon 100mm f/2.8 macro lens
Aperture f/4 | ISO 320 | Shutter speed 1/320 sec

Toads and their young have some interesting defensive mechanisms; if a tadpole is attacked or wounded it releases a substance into the water as a signal to the other tadpoles. As adults they produce a toxin in the skin to deter predators, though a handful of predators are immune to it. Adult toads will also attempt to make themselves more daunting by extending their legs and expanding their bodies. They will also urinate when picked up, which is why if you have ever picked up a toad you may have ended up with wet hands.

Half Submerged

During the daytime smaller male toads can be found in the little stream that runs between ponds in various states of submergence. If you settle in a low down position and watch for a while, they pop their heads up, move around and pop back under the water. I love spending time with these toads and capturing different aspects of their lives. For this image I myself was half submerged in the stream to be at eye level with the toads and watched as they stuck their heads up out of the water and was able to capture this one just as it was coming out of the water seamlessly blending with the flowing water.

Common Toad (*Bufo bufo*)
Canon 5D Mark III with Sigma 180mm f/2.8 macro lens
Aperture f/4 | ISO 200 | Shutter speed 1/160 sec

Unfortunately toad populations have suffered huge declines and a study lead by Froglife found a decline of 68% over the last 30 years in the UK. The study used data from toad patrols that are carried out by volunteers every year as the toads make their migrations to breeding ponds across roads. Hundreds of thousands of toads are moved safely across the roads each spring to carry on their journey to breed, but despite these efforts numbers are still declining. There are several factors that could be contributing to this, including loss of ponds, habitat degradation and fragmentation, increased traffic and climate change. The patrols are often only carried out in spring before the toads breed, but not on the return journey, which is more unpredictable and sporadic, so we all should help by keeping an eye out for toads crossing roads at night time. Once they have bred toads will leave the ponds and head into the surrounding foliage, eventually moving to their hibernation sites.

When I go in search of the toadlets in summer, it is an unhappy sight to see that many are trampled as people aren't aware that they are even there; being so small, people just don't see them, so if you are out and about around known breeding areas, do keep an eye on the ground. If you do see little toadlets, be careful to step around them or give them a helping hand to cross paths to safety.

Eye Of Light

Common toads are most active at night and under the cover of darkness they make the migration from hibernation sites to breeding ponds, although during the breeding season you can often see them during the day. Once the sun sets even more toads start to appear with many sitting in the little stream between the ponds, which is where I found this male. Following a few days of heavy rain, the stream had a lovely movement of water to it. To set up this shot I used an LED panel on a very low setting to light from the side to pick out the eye of the toad and the textures in the water leading up to the eye. Photographing these toads in the stream requires getting wet, a bit chilly, bitten to pieces and mistaken for being a female toad more than once, but it's all worth it to experience and capture this event that lasts just a couple of weeks at most.

Common Toad (*Bufo bufo*)
Canon 5D Mark III with Sigma 180mm f/2.8 macro lens, Manfrotto Lykos LED Panel
Aperture f/3.2 | ISO 500 | Shutter speed 1/640 sec

Puddle Toadlet

Around July time the tiny toadlets (about 1–2cm long) start to emerge from the breeding ponds and make their way into the grasses and surrounding foliage. If you time it just right—after rainfall is a good time—and are really careful with where you step, you can watch these tiny toads crossing the paths. They can be tricky to photograph as they are so small. On a damp day I found a few around a small puddle of water on the path and this one was just poking its head up out of the water.

Common Toad (*Bufo bufo*)
Canon 5D Mark III with Sigma 180mm f/2.8 macro lens
Aperture f/2.8 | ISO 400 | Shutter speed 1/1600sec

Toadlet in the Grass

You can still find toadlets around in August time if you know where to look and especially if you head out on a dewy morning, I found this slightly pink-tinged individual in amongst the grass at the edge of the pond. What really caught my eye with this one was the light coming through the grasses and picking up details in the toad and the dew drops. In addition to the wonderful natural light creating some wonderful patterns, the positioning of the toad compliments the direction of the grasses.

Common Toad (*Bufo bufo*)
Canon 5D Mark III with Sigma 180mm f/2.8 macro lens
Aperture f/4 | ISO 250 | Shutter speed 1/640 sec

Newts

Newts are amphibians with some interesting characteristics. For example, they can regenerate fully functional limbs, organs and tissues. We have three native species of newt in the United Kingdom, the most common one being the smooth newt, and it is the smooth newt that you may come across in the garden, especially if you have a suitable pond for them to breed in.

Smooth newts are predators of slugs, worms and other invertebrates when on land, and shrimp, tadpoles and aquatic invertebrates when in water, making them important natural pest controllers. As food for grass snakes, kingfishers, dragonfly larvae, fish and even other newts, they are an important component of the ecosystem.

In the spring the adults emerge from hibernation, returning to the water to breed. The male performs an elaborate courtship display which involves him vibrating his tail in front of the female, wafting glandular secretions to encourage her approach, after which the male deposits a spermatophore (sperm-containing capsule) in front of the female, who then manoeuvers herself over it to pick it up. After a few days she begins to lays eggs individually, carefully wrapping each one in a leaf.

Hiding In the Leaf Litter

Around the breeding season you can often find newts in the leaf litter surrounding the breeding pond which is where I came across this one whilst carefully sorting and tidying up a few areas surrounding the pond. These animals are full of character and are fun to watch, as I laid on the ground this one kept sticking its head out through the leaves having a look around before disappearing back into the leaves and there is something quite adorable about their faces when seen head on.

Smooth Newt (*Lissotriton vulgaris*)
Canon 30D with Canon 100mm f/2.8 macro lens
Aperture f/7.1 | ISO 320 | Shutter speed 1/100sec

Golden Morning

If you head out in the early morning and there's a heavy dew, you may be lucky enough to come across a newt in the wet grass, which is where I found this individual. It was a particularly wet morning and, whilst looking for damselflies, I came across this newt sitting on a leaf quite out in the open just as the sun was starting to rise, giving a soft, golden-yellow glow to the vegetation while the water droplets added a bit of sparkle to the leaf on which the newt was resting. I used a wide aperture to soften the background, bringing all the attention to the newt which, after a couple of minutes, disappeared into the tall grass.

Smooth Newt (*Lissotriton vulgaris*)
Canon 5D Mark III with Sigma 180mm f/2.8 macro lens
Aperture f/2.8 | ISO 400 | Shutter speed 1/320sec

Reptiles

Reptiles evolved over 300 million years ago. There are six reptile species native to the UK, but just four in my local area, the slow worm, viviparous lizard, European adder and grass snake. All four can often be seen basking as they emerge from hibernation in spring; as ectotherms, they use the warmth from the sun and surrounding habitat to regulate their body temperature. All four species are found in a variety of habitats and all are present at the two larger locations of the four explored in this book. All our reptiles shed their skin, a process known as ecdysis (sloughing), which enables them to grow and shed parasites.

We have only one venomous species in the UK and that is the European adder. They are venomous rather than poisonous as they inject their toxins, the way in which the toxins are delivered determining whether a species is venomous or poisonous. Though the toxins have similar effects once in the body, poisonous animals secrete their toxins rather than inject them, meaning they must be absorbed or ingested.

Slow Worms (*Anguis fragilis*)

Slow worms aren't worms at all, or even snakes, for which they are sometimes mistaken. They are actually legless lizards and, like many lizards, they can shed their tails to escape danger and have eyelids with which they blink. They are most active at dusk, hunting for slow-moving prey such as slugs, making them a friend to gardener; indeed, they can often be found in compost piles. Courtship of these reptiles can last up to 10 hours and appears quite aggressive, with the male biting the neck of the female during intercourse. They are ovoviviparous (the young are incubated in weakly formed eggs, hatching inside the body and then being live born) and take 3-4 years to reach sexual maturity for the males, and 4-5 years for the female.

An Eye In The Dark

Every spring the slow worms come out of hibernation and can occasionally be found basking amongst vegetation if you look carefully. This is where I found this one with the light just catching one side of its head and body on a fairly overcast day. Carefully and slowly I was able to lie on the ground nearby and photograph it head-on with the light just coming in from the side, plunging the other half of the slow worm into shadow as it moved out from the shadows of the surrounding foliage.

Slow Worm (*Anguis fragilis*)
Canon 5D Mark III with Sigma 180mm f/2.8 macro lens
Aperture f/4 | ISO 500 | Shutter speed 1/160sec

Deep In The Shadows

I've often come across slow worms in the shadows curled up in one big mass on overcast and slightly drizzly days. It was on just such a day I managed to captured this image of a slow worm with its head resting on the body of another one in the pile, complete with a couple of water droplets. As you can see, it was a very dull and dreary day, but I don't like to use additional lighting and especially not flash when it comes to reptiles; the darkness adds to the overall feeling of the image.

Slow Worm (*Anguis fragilis*)
Canon 5D Mark III with Sigma 180mm f/2.8 macro lens
Aperture f/4 | ISO 1000 | Shutter speed 1/10sec

Viviparous Lizard (*Zootoca vivipara*)

As with all our reptiles and amphibians, the viviparous or common lizard hibernates over winter to emerge in the spring. They can often be found on fence posts, dry stone walls and walkways basking in the sun. During the breeding season, males will defend their territories from other males and test females' readiness to breed by biting them on the neck; if not ready to mate she will fiercely bite the male. After mating, the young develop inside the female for approximately three months and are then born live, reaching sexual maturity at around 2 years of age for males and three years of age for females. These are quite voracious predators of invertebrates, grabbing their prey and often shaking it before eating it whole.

Afternoon Snooze

If you're patient, quiet and still, you can observe lizards as they go about their lives. One afternoon in late April I found a couple of lizards amongst some building rubble and watched for an hour or so. I was surprised to see one find a sunny spot on stone, close its eyes and appear to snooze for some time, allowing me plenty of time to compose this image with the lizard to the side with its head in focus and its body blurring into the background.

Viviparous Lizard (*Zootoca vivipara*)
Canon 5D Mark III with Sigma 180mm f/2.8 macro lens
Aperture f/5 | ISO 250 | Shutter speed 1/500sec

Feeling Green
Very occasionally I have come across green viviparous lizards at one particular site and it is surprising how much they stand out, especially in amongst the browns of the leaf litter. This is one that was basking on a dead leaf in a position that would allow me to carefully creep up to it and photograph it through the surrounding leaves.

Viviparous Lizard (*Zootoca vivipara*)
Canon 5D Mark III with Canon 100mm f/2.8 macro lens
Aperture f/2.8 | ISO 125 | Shutter speed 1/500sec

European Adder (*Vipera berus*)

The European adder is the United Kingdom's only native venomous snake, but they are not dangerous and are actually quite shy animals. They are both beautiful and fascinating snakes, hibernating over the winter with the males emerging first, normally around March, but I have seen males basking as early as the beginning of February in warmer years. When they first emerge they will spend the first few weeks basking to enable sperm production (spermatogenesis), ready for the coming breeding season, and within a few weeks they will slough their skin to reveal the beautiful silver and black colouration that is often associated with adders. At this point they will start to search for females (which emerge roughly a month later) using scent trails. After mating, the male will guard the female for a couple of days and, if another male attempts to mate with the female, they may perform an incredible battle known as the "Dance of the Adders". If you see this, it is actually two males battling rather than a male and female. Females only breed every couple of years and although they reach sexual maturity at around 3 years of age, they may not breed successfully until the age of 8 years. Males, on the other hand, reach sexual maturity around the age of 3 years.

In recent years adders have become something of a photographic trophy species and although people wanting to see and photograph these beautiful snakes is encouraging, there is often little consideration for the potential damage they maybe causing in the pursuit of an image. All my images are taken *in situ* where the snakes are basking and from a safe distance so as not to disturb them, but unfortunately there are many that cause disturbance by getting too close, resulting in the snakes going into hiding so that they are not able to make the most of basking opportunities; others will catch and position them in clean habitats away from their usual haunts. These practises could have profound effects on the breeding success and therefore future generations of adders. So please do be careful and respectful, and do a little research before attempting to photograph them in the wild. This is true of all amphibians and reptiles.

Face-Off

Very occasionally you have an encounter with wildlife that you never expected, but which stays with you forever; this was one such encounter. I had seen this male out basking by a tussock of grass and found myself a position a safe distance away so as not to disturb him, mostly to observe and possibly take photographs. As I lay there amongst the very potent stinging nettles, he started to come out into the open a little more and I was able to capture him face on as his head came through the grass. I had enough time as I laid there, almost motionless, to experiment with the aperture, getting the eyes in focus but leaving the surroundings blurred; as I slowly backed away, so as not to disturb him, he was still basking and making the most of the warm spring sunshine. This is an encounter that will always have a place in my heart, proving that these really are placid, beautiful and often misunderstood animals.

European Adder (*Vipera berus*)
Canon 5D Mark III with Sigma 180mm f/2.8 macro lens
Aperture f/5 | ISO 400 | Shutter speed 1/800sec

Perfect Camouflage

I have often found adders basking in small open areas amongst the old gorse bushes, but they can be tricky to spot unless they move. I know of a couple of males that favour such a spot and it was only because one of them repositioned himself that I actually saw him. They are almost perfectly camouflaged in this habitat with the dabbled light and shadows breaking up their outline. Carefully crouching down I was able to find a small opening through which I could just about see his head and more importantly his eye on which is the point of focus. I really wanted to illustrate just how well camouflaged these snakes can be whilst also showing them in their habitat, using a wide aperture to soften the surrounding vegetation really drawing the focus to his eye deep within the gorse bush.

European Adder (*Vipera berus*)
Canon 7D with Sigma 120-300mm f/2.8 Sports Lens
Aperture f/4 | ISO 320 | Shutter speed 1/2000sec

Perfect Miniature

Adders are viviparous meaning they give birth to live young. The young are incubated inside the female through the summer months making thermoregulation essential for the development of the young. Baby snakes (neonates) are born ready to fend for themselves in late summer and are perfect miniatures of the adults. These little adders live off fat reserves over winter and won't feed until the following spring, if you're lucky you may see the neonates in the autumn, but often you will see them the following spring when they emerge to bask, which is when I was lucky enough to photograph this one. The neonates are about pencil-sized with all the character of the adults including tiny venom glands and tiny fangs, but they are without doubt much more adorable.

European Adder (*Vipera berus*)
Canon 5D Mark III with Canon 100mm f/2.8 macro lens
Aperture f/4 | ISO 400 | Shutter speed 1/320sec

Grass Snake (*Natrix natrix*)

Grass snakes are the longest snake found in the United Kingdom and they are non-venomous. They feed primarily on amphibians and fish and can occasionally be found in or around garden ponds. 'Natrix' comes from the Latin meaning "to swim" and they are very good swimmers. The grass snake is our only egg-laying snake species, and it uses rotting vegetation or even compost heaps to lay in the early summer; perfect miniature baby grass snakes hatch out in late summer. Although harmless, the grass snake may coil in a defensive behaviour and hiss loudly if cornered. They may also feign death and, if handled, exude a foul smelling liquid.

Curled Up

Male grass snake curled up basking in the warm spring sunshine. I have converted this to monochrome to highlight the patterns of the scales and coils.

Grass snake (*Natrix natrix*)
Canon 5D Mark III with Canon 100mm f/2.8 macro lens
Aperture f/4.5 | ISO 400 | Shutter speed 1/800 sec

Flick of the Tongue

A large female individual, one of the largest I've seen, on a mound of grass next to the gorse and heather flicking her tongue with the reflection of the sky in her eye. Snakes flick their tongues to collect chemical information from their environment in the form of tiny, moisture-borne particles. These particles are deposited in the mouth and transferred to the Jacobson's or vomeronasal organ allowing the snake to detect both mates and prey.

Grass snake (*Natrix natrix*)
Canon 5D Mark III with Canon 100mm f/2.8 macro lens
Aperture f/2.8 | ISO 640 | Shutter speed 1/1250sec

References

Blamey M., Fitter R. & Fitter A. 2013. *Wild Flowers of Britain and Ireland.* Bloomsbury Natural History.

Chinery M. 2012. *Insects of Britain and Western Europe.* A&C Black.

Futahashi R. 2016. Color vision and color formation in dragonflies. *Current Opinion in Insect Science* Vol. 17, October, pp 32–39.

Ghazanfar M., Malik M.F., Hussain M., Iqbal R. and Younas M. 2016. Butterflies and Their Contribution in Ecosystem: A Review. *Journal of Entomology and Zoology Studies* 4(2): 115-118.

Gullan P.J. & Cranston P.S. 2000. *The Insects: An Outline of Entomology* (2nd Ed). Blackwell Science.

Noel, A.C., Guo H-Y., Mandica M. and Hu D.L. 2017: http://physicsworld.com/cws/article/news/2017/feb/01/frogs-use-non-newtonian-saliva-to-capture-prey

Petrovan, S. O., & Schmidt, B. R. 2016. Volunteer Conservation Action Data Reveals Large-Scale and Long-Term Negative Population Trends of a Widespread Amphibian, the Common Toad (*Bufo bufo*). PLoS ONE, *11*(10), e0161943. http://doi.org/10.1371/journal.pone.0161943

Pough, F. Harvey, Robin M. Andrews, John E. Cadle, Martha L. Crump, Alan H. Savitzky, and Kentwood D. Wells. 2001. *Herpetology,* Second Edition. New York: Prentice Hall.

Prum, R.O., Quinn T. and Torres R.H. 2006. Anatomically diverse butterfly scales all produce structural colours by coherent scattering. *The Journal of Experimental Biology* 209, pp748-765.

Smallshire D. & Swash A. 2014. *Britain's Dragonflies: A field guide to the damselflies and dragonflies of Britain and Ireland.* Princeton University Press.

Thomas J. and Lewington R. 2014. *The Butterflies of Britain and Ireland.* British Wildlife Publishing.

Zeng J, Xiang N, Jiang L, Jones G, Zheng Y *et al.* 2011. Moth Wing Scales Slightly Increase the Absorbence of Bat Echolocation Calls. *PLoS ONE* 6(11): e27190.

http://voices.nationalgeographic.com/2013/06/14/the-pink-grasshopper-no-its-not-a-cocktail/

Reference Websites

http://www.mendiphillsaonb.org.uk/

https://www.wiltshirewildlife.org/

http://www.somersetwildlife.org/

http://www.english-nature.org.uk/citation/citation_photo/1002573.pdf

https://www.buglife.org.uk/

https://www.woodlandtrust.org.uk/

http://butterfly-conservation.org/

http://www.learnaboutbutterflies.com/